BEST BRA1

BRAIN SPRINTS

What They're Saying...

Ed Mayhew is a master of movement learning. His brain sprints get students up and moving with fun and purposeful activities. The brain sprints get students heart rate up thus allowing students to return to academic work ready to focus. If you want achievement to improve, get students moving with a practical approach.

— Dr. Mark Y. Lineburg,
Superintendent, Halifax Co.

Ed shared his passion for physical activity and "Brain Sprints" at our VAESP [Virginia Association of Elementary School Principals] Northern Zone meeting. He had some of the best and brightest principals in the area jogging, jumping and actively engaged in learning. His data on the correlation between brain activity and physical activity reinforced what we have observed as educators – kids need stimulation to motivate and connect learning. We had a blast! Thanks for sharing how Mega Brain-Power Boosters leads to smarter, stronger children.

— Clark Bowers, Ed.D. Northern
Zone Director for VAESP

Ed Mayhew's *Mega Brain Power Boosters / Brain Sprints* program was well received by the attendees at the VAESP Annual conference. His session was energetic, engaging and well received by the conference participants. All left with new ideas on how best to liven up instruction and promote academic success.

— Jim Baldwin, Executive Director,
Virginia Association of Elementary School Principals
(VAESP)

Ed Mayhew has been coming to my classroom for years to lead Brain Sprints! The students love combining movement and the math curriculum! They are effective and FUN! We love the Brain Man!

— Michele Ambrogi, 3rd grade teacher,
Winchester Public Schools

Ed Mayhew's Mega Brain Power Boosters/Brain Sprints program is awesome for our Elementary Students at VACDES. Our students enjoy learning as they move to the rhythm and beats that Ed teaches them. Math and Moving is fun, Ed Mayhew's way. I highly recommend his program. As a Physical Education Teacher for 45 years, I have seen how he really gets our students pumped up to learn various academic subjects.

— Shelly Lee, P.E. Teacher Pre-K -4th Grade

Over the past 10 years I have used Mr. Mayhew's strategies and activities to support my language arts and math curriculum. His research-based strategies get my students exercising and keep them motivated all while learning math and reading skills.

— Cassy Roark, Elementary School Teacher

Thank you for your book. It is a wealth of information. It is not only handy for teachers, but parents, too. I would love for you to visit my classroom...especially like your addressing ADHD.

— Martha Smith, Teacher

The connection between mind and body is both intuitive and scientifically proven. Ed Mayhew brings proven, simple solutions to the classroom and school environment to ensure that the seven hours we have with children each day include body-mind activity.

— Dr. Jason Van Heukelum, Superintendent
Winchester Public Schools, VA

Ed Mayhew's Mega Brain Power Boosters / Brain Sprints activities were well received by our staff and students. His program of activities are important reminders of the link between physical activity, movement, and learning.

— Andrew Buchheit,
Elementary School Principal

I have worked in education with Ed Mayhew for over twenty-five years. Brain Sprints is an engaging program that makes learning fun, active and effective.

— Tina Genay,
Elementary School Librarian

As a long-time elementary school principal, I've seen firsthand what Ed Mayhew's Mega Brain Power Boosters can do. They flat-out work!

— J. Vernon Laney,
Curriculum Coordinator

Your contributions in educating our student body on the importance of physical activity in brain development were very well received. You did an excellent job varying the single assembly to a wide range of students from grades kindergarten to 8th grade. As a faculty, we would like for you to return and share more of your techniques to enhance our teaching.

— Janie Lyman, 4th grade teacher,
Sacred Heart Academy

"I like doing brain sprints. We all like doing it. It's really fun..." * "Thank you for being the best teacher forever. We love you Mr. Mayhew..." * "Thank you for teaching us brain sprints... it made me better at math, reading..." * "Brain man I like the way you teach. It is so cool..." * "I love your aktivde. [sic] They are so fun. They are the funest [sic] thing in school. *

— Students' written comments

I think you hit the jackpot! What an excellent interview, and the examples certainly made it interesting. I bet every parent will want to buy this book . I will tell all my friends with children.

— Hilde Matheson, counselor,
parent & grandparent

Thank you very much for presenting the Mega Brain Power Boosters Program for Excellence to the faculty last week. The strategies that you modeled combined academic content with large-muscle movement and are great for use in the classroom.

— *Michele Dempsey, principal,*
Virginia Avenue Elementary School

I would highly recommend Mr. Mayhew as a presenter. He shares research information and personal experiences from his [50-year] teaching career that support the relationship between learning and exercise...

— *Rebecca McTavish, principal,*
Sacred Heart Academy

The "Brain Sprints" are a great addition to my teacher's "tool bag." They reinforce the children's learning and give them a short movement break at the same time.

— *Sandy and Dick Widell, Teachers,*
Parents & Grandparents

I highly recommend Ed Mayhew's Mega Brain Power Boosters / Brain Sprints program. It was well received by the students, teachers and parents alike...it is an easy and fun way to accelerate academic learning...

— *Anita Jenkins,*
Elementary School Principal

Thanks Ed! I do the Supercharger [a Brain Sprints essential] exercise with whatever we happen to be doing – sometimes we just do the alphabet! The kids always feel their hearts beating afterwards and I tell them to feel their brains growing, too! It's quick and easy – it makes sense!

— Laura Baker—Anderle,
First Grade Teacher / Team Leader

Mega Brain Boosters is supported by research that confirms that physical activity strengthens neural connections. We have been very pleased to utilize Ed Mayhew's Brain Sprints Program in our school.

— Nan K. Bryant, Ed.D. Principal
Virginia Avenue Charlotte DeHart
Elementary School

Thank you so much [for presentation to fifth-grade staff]. I know it was a success because several teachers used the strategies you taught them today and it was great. I would love to have you back in a couple of months.

— Lisa Cobb, Assistant Principal

Thank you so much for coming to ISWI. We were thrilled with the information and plan for action that you presented. I heard many positive comments from the faculty. Diane, who is a Jazzercise instructor...and Meghan, who is very athletic, were both especially excited about implementing the program in their classrooms. We will begin tomorrow. We are very interested in the dual goals of promoting physical health and preparing young brains for maximum receptivity to learning. *10 months later in an email –* Hope your business is booming. Our students have benefitted tremendously!

— Claire McDonald, Ph.D., Head of School, The Independent School of Winchester, Inc.

Ed Mayhew has the ability to reach all ages and abilities in his demonstrations which stimulate the brain as well as the body. His explanations about what is going on in the brain and body are succinct and readily understandable. His demonstrations are interspersed with his humor. Ed has done several sessions for our retiree group and everyone enjoys his work.

— Ben McCartney, President Virginia Retired Teachers Association

What They're Saying About Some of Ed's Other Books...

Age Blasters: 3 Steps to a Younger You

Fitter After 50

Fitter for Life

Recently been thinking about retiring from running [competitively]. However, after reading that book [Ed Mayhew's *Fitter for Life*] I'm all inspired about keeping on with running.

> — *Age-Group World Champion ultra-marathon runner Helen Klein, 81, went on to run the Lake Tahoe Triple (a marathon a day for 3 consecutive days) just shy of her 82nd birthday*

"Your book [*Fitter After 50*] has just the right touch. I have given it to many friends in hope that they will improve their lives."

> — *Ken "Ice" Morrison, 65-year-old hockey player*

Ed Mayhew [will] definitely exercise your laugh muscles with funny anecdotes and an infectious enthusiasm.

> — *Randy Bryant, attorney at law*

I would love to have you on again . I will keep you in mind, and definitely plan to have you back soon.

— Steve Wall, host of "Deep Thoughts"
radio show on KEZW, Denver

I LOVE getting your newsletter!! This was just so inspiring!!! Great stuff!!!!

— Susan Duvall, publicity director,
The Health & Wellness Center
by Doylestown Hospital

Ed Mayhew is a delightful and entertaining speaker. He made me smile and think at the same time. I would recommend him as a speaker to any organization.

— Steve M. Gyurisin,
Frederick County Rotary Club

It is really an inspiration to read about all those people in the book [Ed Mayhew's *Fitter After 50*]. It makes me want to set some high goals."

— Wallace Rapozo, Masters Biathlete

"All of us were inspired by your presentation. Your humor was such a treat. Yours [talk] was definitely the best of the entire convocation!"

— Brooke Hill, Guidance &
Counseling Department Head

Ed, you are an inspiration to me. Your book and presentation stoked a fire inside. Bottom line: Keep up the good work! You're right on target."

— Jack Recker, Business Manager

Your book [*Fitter for Life*] is excellent! It's interesting, fun to read and full of great information and inspiration, not just for the health 'beginner', but for all of us who have been 'at it' for years as well. Great job!"

— Marguerite Meyer, 46,
American Champion age-group swimmer

All these profiles [in *Fitter for Life*] have one thing in common. They prove that anyone, regardless of their age or circumstances, can become healthier and happier and can slow the aging process by simply becoming more active. It is simply a matter of the right attitude, and with the right attitude, anyone can do it.

— Laura Val, multi-time
World Champion age-group swimmer

"I got 5 or 6 compliments on your [radio interview] presentation on Laura Val this past week."

— Kristin Farson,
Host of the Better Times radio show

BEST BRAIN BREAKS EVER

BRAIN SPRINTS

Mega Brain-Power Boosting
for Classroom & Home

ED MAYHEW

LUMINARE PRESS
WWW.LUMINAREPRESS.COM

Printed in the United States of America

Cover Design: Luminare Press

Luminare Press
442 Charnelton St.
Eugene, OR 97401
www.luminarepress.com

ISBN: 978-1-64388-216-1
LCCN: 2019911942

This book is dedicated to all the wonderful teachers and children who invited me into their classrooms. They, with their energetic and joyful participation, let me know that my Brain Sprints truly are the Best Brain Breaks Ever!

Table of Contents

Chapter Three

Chapter Four

Chapter Five

Chapter Six

Chapter Seven

Chapter Eight

Introduction

THE HOW AND WHY OF BRAIN SPRINTS

"The point I've tried to make – that [aerobic] exercise is the single most powerful tool you have to optimize your brain function – is based on evidence I've gathered from hundreds and hundreds of research papers..."

—John Ratey, MD and author of
Spark: The Revolutionary New Science
of Exercise and the Brain

Brain Sprints is a treasure trove of activities to greatly improve the cognition and overall well-being of our children. Whether you are a teacher, tutor, parent, grandparent or other adult, you are encouraged to refer to this book often for science-based activities that will boost the brain-power and well-being of your youngsters.

These mega brain-power boosters, most of the time, combine academic subject matter of the adult's choice with light, moderate and/or vigorous-intensity physical activities. The academics are joined with the physical activities / exercises because for two decades neuroscientists have been finding and telling us through their experiments that aerobic exercise is either the most important or one of the most important ways to significantly improve the structure and function of the brain.

These Brain Sprints and other mega brain-power boosters have been tested and proven in dozens and dozens of classrooms and with hundreds of delighted students and their teachers. Only the best brain-boosting activities are included in this book; those that weren't that effective and well received were left on the cutting-room floor.

Why Introduce Movement Activities into the Classroom

Those of us with a little more grey hair remember a time when we would play outside for hours. Our parents would send us out with the admonition to come home when the street lights came on, often not knowing where we would be in the neighborhood or the town – nor what we would be doing.

Instead of going outside to play, too many of today's kids entertain themselves in front of screens of various sizes. In most neighborhoods, it's safe to say, it is unusual to see youngsters outside playing even on the most beautiful of days. They are happy to be inside unknowingly developing an unhealthy, sedentary brain-numbing lifestyle.

Here are a couple of stories to back up the above assertion. The other day while strolling down the hallway of an elementary school, I stopped to look at the samples of schoolwork posted on the walls. The second graders had been asked to write about what they do on a snow day. This seven-year-old whose paper caught my eye said, "I watch videos on YouTube all day and then play on PlayStation with Dad." Isn't it a virtual indictment against today's technology-centered childhood that she did not say anything about building snowmen, sledding, doing angels in the snow or having snowball fights or having other fun in the snow?

Yours truly spends a lot of time in elementary school classrooms doing Brain Sprints activities with the classes. One game is called *This OR That*. In this activity the students jog in place beside their desks to some lively music while listening to me giving them two choices. Once they've heard both options, they jump up three times, each time saying out loud their choice. One such choice is: "Would you rather stay inside and play a video game OR go outside and play tag?' In classroom after classroom, the overwhelming retort is, "Video game! Video game! Video game!"

Now let's look at some statistics and analyses that seem to back up this view that today's kids are not getting the exercise they need to be their best physically, mentally, emotionally and socially.

- A mere 43% of US kids, ages 6 to 11, met the recommended 60-minutes-most-days activity level (2016 National Physical Activity Plan Alliance report card)

- Only 42% of a sampling of treadmill-tested American children were deemed aerobically fit – down from 52% about a decade earlier (2014 CDC report)

- The guideline of no more than 2 hours per day of screen time was met by a mere 47% of youngsters ages 6 to 11 and even less by teens (2016 NPAPA report card)

- According to the "Beep test" / 20-meter shuttle run test of cardiovascular fitness, American 12-year-olds ranked 37th out of 40 countries tested (2016 analysis by Grant Tomkinson, University of North Dakota)

- "Physical activity and cardiovascular fitness are good for children's and young people's brain development and function as well as their intellect." (Consensus Statement: The Copenhagen Consensus Conference, 2016)

The Science Connecting MVPA to Cognition

Here is a little of what researchers have found in recent years concerning what aerobic exercise does to improve brain power:

1. Increases levels of Brain-Derived Neurotrophic Factor (BDNF) in the hippocampus (learning & memory), resulting in neurogenesis – the growth of new neurons

2. Increases the size and number of mitochondria (the cells' power plants) in brain cells

3. Levels of glutamate (by far the number one excitatory neurotransmitter) are increased in the visual cortex and the anterior cingulate cortex (cognition and emotions)

4. Releases endorphins and endocannabinoids in the brain, which produce a natural high that improves readiness to learn

5. Unleashes Human Growth Hormone (Hgh) which signals the release of a number of growth factors in and into the brain to grow new brain cells and the capillaries to support them (which significantly assists learning)

Among the discoveries University scientists have made is that aerobically-fit youngsters tend to have:

- Larger hippocampi (learning & memory) and basal ganglia (executive control – ability to stay focused and on task in class)
- More white matter which connects different parts of the brain
- More neural connections in the prefrontal lobes (thinking, decision making...)

A study of 1.2 million Swedish military recruits over several decades found a strong correlation between the aerobic fitness of the young men and their IQ. This link held for the thousands of pairs of twins in the study which means it isn't likely to be the result of genetics or upbringing, but rather the cardiovascular fitness of the recruits. In addition, those individuals who improved their aerobic fitness between the ages of 15 and 18 also tended to have improvement in their cognition. No similar correlation was found for the strength fitness component (University of Gothenburg, 2009).

Exercise Improves Academics

Here are some of the university study findings concerning the connection between moderate-to-vigorous physical activity and learning and academic achievement.

- A SINGLE 12-minute session of running-in-place improved reading comprehension scores of college-age students from low-income families by a whopping 17% (Dartmouth College, 2014)
- A single twenty-minute walk by elementary-age students increased reading comprehension scores an

average of ONE WHOLE GRADE LEVEL (University of Illinois, 2010)

- Doubling physical education from two to four hours per week "DOUBLED THE ODDS" that fifth graders in Sweden reached the national learning goals in Swedish, English and math (Sahlgrenska Academy, 2014)

- Two-hour daily afterschool program "...improved two-fold" elementary students' accuracy and speed on cognitive tasks (University of Illinois, 2014)

- One 30-second all-out sprint on a stationary bike increased human growth hormone (Hgh) 530% above baseline (University of Loughborough, 2002); a 10—second all-out sprint at the end of a moderate-intensity 20-minute bike ride stabilized blood-sugar levels in type 1 diabetics and unleased Hgh (Hgh activates the growth factors, such as BDNF, necessary for learning and memory) Western Australia University, 2006

The Solution

Kids' bodies and brains were designed to need a lot of Moderate-to-Vigorous Physical Activity (MVPA) to develop optimally. Even with PE classes, recess and the *opportunity* to participate in a host of sports leagues, dance studios, martial arts clubs, etc., most of our kids are still not getting the minimal recommended daily 60 minutes of MVPA. And, it gets worse as they move into their teens, with only an estimated 7.5% of them getting the recommended amount of physical activity, according to the 2016 NPAP report card.

This is where occasional Brain Sprints sessions in the classroom and at home can come to the rescue. Children, especially elementary-age youngsters and younger, spend the bulk of their day in the classroom at school and before and after school at home. These two places are where we can reach the most kids.

Imagine if several times each school day the teacher had the students enjoy a five-to-ten-minutes Brain Sprints session. Then when at home, what if their parents had them do a couple of brief sessions, too? Let's say they do four 5-minute Brain Sprints at school and two at home – that would be 30 minutes of MVPA or about half of what is recommended. Then they can get the rest at recess, in physical education class, at soccer practice and in backyard play. How likely is it that when all these "exercise" sessions are added up that they would be getting all the daily MVPA they need to be their best? What if the Brain Sprints sessions at school and home were 10 minutes long? How likely then would it be that their brain and body are ready to develop optimally?

In addition to getting their daily quota of exercise, the Brain Sprints sessions at school and home are likely developing a lifelong habit of taking brain-power-boosting, overall-well-being-enhancing exercise breaks throughout their day. And we haven't even mentioned how a lifelong active lifestyle would greatly improve the odds of their staying well and cutting healthcare costs way down in their adult years. Researchers for a 2017 Johns Hopkins University / Bloomberg School of Public Health, using a computer-generated model, projected that the cost of our current sedentary 8-to-11-year-olds will be a staggering "2.8 Trillion [yes, that is a 'T'] in additional medical costs and lost wages over their lifetimes." That doesn't even take into consideration the human suffering and misery. What good is it to teach kids math, reading and history if we don't teach them and model for them an active lifestyle and how to get it. Making Brain Sprints in the classroom and at home a regular occurrence is a major step to making MVPA a lifelong habit, and a healthy, happy life more of a certainty.

Your Children and the Brain Sprints Advantage

The Brain Sprints and the many mega brain-power booster activities under its *umbrella* in the pages that follow greatly improve the structure/function of the brain and improve academic achievement because of the following attributes and components.

Engages Visual, Auditory, Tactile/Kinesthetic SIMULTANEOUSLY

Most of the activities in the chapters to follow engage all the major modes of learning at the same time. Whether a child is predominantly a visual learner, an auditory learner or a tactile/kinesthetic one or needs to vocalize to learn best, his learning needs are met AND supplemented by the additional modes of learning. This fires up the associated brain regions (i.e. the visual cortex, Broca and Wernicke Areas, motor cortex, hippocampus, prefrontal cortex, etc.) for improved thinking and storage and retrieval of information.

Boosts Brain-Power through MVPA

The Moderate-to-Vigorous Physical Activity (MVPA) component of the Brain Sprints boosts brain-power by improving the structure/function of the brain. University studies have shown that a SINGLE brief bout of exercise (i.e. MVPA) can significantly improve recall, selective visual attention, math skills and reading comprehension.

Over time, by regularly sprinkling these MVPA-rich brain-power boosters into the whole days' activities, your youngsters will become much more aerobically fit. University research has found that fit children tend to have greater white matter integrity, larger hippocampi, better cognition and higher standardized academic test scores. In this regard, as a result of his team's research, Francisco B. Ortega reported, "...physical [aerobic] fitness is linked in a direct way to important brain structure differences and such differences are reflected in the children's academic performance." *2018 University of Granada study*

A study published in *Frontiers in Neuroscience* in 2018, found that limiting weight-bearing exercise involving the legs decreased neural stem cells in the brain by 70 percent and negatively affected the cells' mitochondria; these stem cells are necessary for neurogenesis (the birthing of new neurons – new brain cells in the learning and memory part of the brain). Although the subjects were mice, the scientists felt that humans (our kids) would experience similar deleterious effects from a lack of sufficient weight-bearing exercise. The running-in-place and jumping components of the Brain Sprints assures that the youngsters get plenty of the weight-bearing exercise that helps power their brains.

The result of our kids getting plenty of moderate and vigorous activity (think: Brain Sprints, here) is also the unleashing of a virtual flood of brain-power-boosting chemicals in their brains and into their brains. Here's a very incomplete list:

Human Growth Hormone (Hgh – signals growth factors for body and brain)
Fibroblast Growth Factor (FGF-2 – needed for cell division to grow new brain cells and capillaries needed to supply oxygen and nutrients to them)

Brain-Derived Neurotrophic Factor (BDNF – Miracle Grow for the brain)

Atrial Natriuretic Peptide (ANP – reduces learning-inhibiting stress)

Nitric Oxide (NO – dilates blood vessels for more oxygenated blood to brain)

Cathepsin B (released by muscles during exercise and travels to brain, where it is needed for neurogenesis in hippocampus)

Noggin (Blocks BMP so that stem cells in hippocampus can turn into full-fledged neurons)

Osteocalcin (produced by the bones and travels to the brain where it is needed for learning and memory)

Irisin (A by-product of muscle contraction that travels to the brain where it increases BDNF in hippocampus)

Glutamate (#1 excitatory neurotransmitter – with 8 to 20 minutes of MVPA it fires up the brain and is increased in the visual cortex and the anterior cingulate cortex (memory, emotions & heart rate)

Remember, these are just a few of the many learning-enhancing bio-chemicals that are unleashed in and into the brain when our youngsters (or we) engage in moderate-to-vigorous physical exercise. Brain Sprints learning-activities can supply a daily healthy dose of moderate-to-vigorous physical activity.

Supplies the Novelty on Which the Brain Thrives

The brain loves the new and different. How many hours did we spend sitting in a classroom while growing up and how many of those thousands of hours do we remember? The answer is: not many, because the same-old, same-old is soon forgotten. These unique physical activities combined with academic material make Brain Sprints a *novel* way – a memorable way -- to learn.

Engages the Emotions

There's a reason the brain's hippocampus has two very different parts. There's a learning and memory section (dorsal) and an emotional part (ventral). That's because we need to involve the emotions in order to remember information and events. The more emotion connected with the event/information, the better we remember it. Brain Sprints are fun and an exciting change from the humdrum seated activities of the typical classroom. The whole class jumping up and down, for example, and enthusiastically saying out loud their answers several times, is going to be remembered much better than one child's being called upon to give the answer while the others are listening (or NOT).

Utilizes Repetition

Many of the Brain Sprints activities use repetition to strengthen the neural circuits for the information being learned. It's the reason, when we meet someone new, that we use their name in the ensuing conversation or repeat it mentally a few times. Repetition is necessary to retain information. The brain doesn't waste energy and resources maintaining circuitry for information that we haven't repeated or have never revisited after hearing/seeing it once or twice.

Teacher's/Parent's Choice of Subject Matter

The teacher, parent or grandparent, in most cases, gets to choose what specific academic subject matter is combined with the science-based brain-power-boosting physical activity of each Brain Sprints session.

Getting to choose the academic component means that the lesson can be specially tailored to the specific needs of the class or individual student. And unlike the many videos for the classroom, where the content, often lacking any academic value, is locked in, the Brain Sprints allow for the instructor to make changes on the fly when needed. The major exception to this is the Brain Sprints math videos which come with a basic math fact lesson already included.

No Expensive Equipment or Program to Buy

In contrast to the need to purchase a big ball for each student to sit on, peddle-desks for entire classes or expensive programs, implementing the Brain Sprints into your curriculum takes little or no investment. Other than the costs associated with displaying the lesson on the Smartboard, dry-erase board or flip chart, there is usually no expense. A rare few lessons call for balls to be tossed, but these can be borrowed from the PE department, purchased at the dollar store or made from balled up newspaper and tape.

Easily Fit Right in the Classroom or Home

Most of these brain-power-boosting activities can be performed in the classroom right next to the students' desks or at home. For almost all the Brain Sprints not a single desk or piece of furniture needs to be moved out of the way. These fun and valuable learning sessions are extremely easy to implement and therefore, most teachers and parents find them easy to use. Because of the ease of implementation, most teachers and parents will actually use these brain-power boosters on a regular basis and therefore, the kids will get a huge learning advantage – THE BRAIN SPRINTS ADVANTAGE!

Myelinates the Axons of the Corpus Callosum

One of the basic movements in the world of Brain Sprints is the *Supercharger*. This movement has several variations. The most basic one has the performer marching in place and alternately touching the raised knee with the opposing hand (i.e. the right hand touches the raised left knee and then the left hand touches the raised right knee).

You would think this would be easy for all school-aged youngsters, but you would be wrong. The Supercharger is initially "impossible to do" for many kindergartners and first graders. You can show them repeatedly how to move their limbs to do this activity while explaining it to them and they will not be able to do it. You can even physically manipulate their limbs so that they are doing this cross-lateral movement with your help, but as soon as you let go they will go right back to touching the right knee with the right hand and the left knee with the left hand.

Note: When introducing the *Supercharger* to young children, we'll show how to use stickers to greatly and easily speed up the learning process for this very potent activity.

The reason for some children's inability to do this seemingly simple task is that the communication and coordination between the two brain hemispheres is weak. We will show you how to easily teach the *Supercharger* so that its practice thereafter will strengthen the *corpus callosum* – the neuronal "bridge" that connects the brain hemispheres. The reason this is important is because the two hemispheres are specialists and need to work together for optimal performance. The left hemisphere (for most of us), for example, houses the language areas of the brain and reads/deciphers the written words; the right hemisphere does most of the reading comprehension. When the hemispheres are strongly linked, the student can figure out and read the words while following the "story" at the same time. With poor linkage they may be able to read the words, but not be able to comprehend very well what has been read.

Repeated use of the *Supercharger* actually increases the myelination of axons in the Corpus Callosum - turning neural pathways into neural superhighways, so to speak - while improving the connection, coordination and communication between the hemispheres.

How to Use This Book

Brain Sprints is meant to be a reference and instruction book. You can use it to find activities you would like to try with your class or child. If you find a Brain Sprints activity beneficial for your needs and the needs of your children, you can add it to your cache of valuable teaching tools. As a discerning individual, you are not supposed to love every activity, but if you stick with it, you are sure to find several that you and your youngsters like and which help them learn. Please don't let me keep you; dive right in and find your first Brain Sprints lesson and ENJOY!

CHAPTER ONE

Jog, Jump 'n Learn

"Single sessions of and long-term participation in physical activity improve cognitive performance and brain health. Children who [regularly] participate in vigorous- or moderate-intensity physical activity benefit the most."

—National Academy of Medicine
panel report, 2013

These super fun activities are sure to more fully engage your youngsters in the learning at hand. This is partly because they involve the visual, auditory, tactile/kinesthetic and vocalization modes of learning SIMULTANEOUSLY! The more senses involved in the learning, the better the recall.

Alternating between the moderate physical activity of jogging in place and the more vigorous activity of jumping, *Jog, Jump 'n Learn* supplies the brain-power-boosting benefits of aerobic exercise. Add to this the fact that they can be performed right next to students' desks, right in the classroom or at home, and we have a winner.

The emotions of joy and excitement the active students are likely to feel make remembering the academic component much more likely. The learning and memory parts of the brain thrive on the new, the different and combining jogging and jumping with math, reading and other academic subject matter certainly supplies that novelty.

Following are several *Jog, Jump 'n Learn* learning activities. Try them, modify them to best meet your and your students' needs and ability levels. Remember that your enthusiasm is important, too. Put on some upbeat music and actively/joyfully participate with your kids. With regular use, these mega-brain-power-boosting activities in this chapter and the rest of the book are sure to greatly improve your kids' academic achievement and overall well-being.

Finally, as my father taught me many years ago, always leave them wanting more. Keep these mega-brain-power-boosting sessions short, i.e., from one to five minutes each. Start with shorter one-to-two-minute activity sessions and increase as the students' endurance increases, as it naturally will with consistent use. For later 10-minute bouts combine two different Brain Sprints, such as a *Jog, Jump 'n Learn* activity from this chapter with one from *Racing in the Classroom* (chapter 7), for example.

Jump for Joy

A Great Start to the New School Year, Each Week...

Purpose:

To practice & improve reading skills, to provide a brain-power-boosting brain break, a powerful mood booster, the ability to express themselves, and/or readiness to focus & learn

Grades:

Preschool to fifth grade and up depending on the youngster(s) or group (e.g., groups of adults greatly enjoy this, too) – not a reading activity for youngest

Duration:

One to five minutes – always keep them wanting more

Equipment Needed:

A numbered list of 10 to 20 open-ended statements displayed on a SMART board, dry-erase board, flip chart...For Example:

1. A food I like to eat IS _____!

2. My favorite game to play when inside IS _____!

3. A person I'd like to spend more time with IS _____!

Other possibilities: flavor of ice cream, place, school subject, color, pet, wild animal, sport, outside game, book or story, drink, vegetable, fruit, dessert, sports team, toy, holiday, cartoon, superhero, favorite thing did during summer vacation, snow activity, best personal quality, when I grow up, _____, _____, _____!

Note: Jump for Joy chart supplied at end of chapter.

How To:

Have students jog in place beside their desks continuously throughout the *Jog, Jump 'n Joy* session, except for the interludes of jumping. While they jog, have them read (or repeat after you) the statements out loud and in unison. Right after they say the word "is," they jump up three times quickly in succession. At the top of each jump they clap their hands overhead a single time and say their unique answer. For example, they jog while reading/saying, "A food I like IS" and then immediately jump up three times saying, "pizza, pizza, pizza!" OR "broccoli, broccoli, broccoli!" In this example, they would say broccoli or pizza once with each jump.

Tips:

Before starting, go over any words or statements with which you think the class might have trouble. Actively participate as leader for the class or pick a student leader. If and while a student is leading, point to each word as it is being read. To more fully engage them visually, skip from statement number 1 to statement number 4 and back to 2, for example. Put on some upbeat music and encourage them to jump energetically/powerfully to get the most from the activity. Optional: Follow up this activity with a discussion of their favorite answers and/or write or draw a picture concerning them.

Modify to meet your needs or the needs of individual students. For example, a student in a wheelchair can pump her arms like she's running and clap her hands overhead during the jumping action.

Jump for Joy is the perfect activity to start each week or to use when returning from a lengthy time off, such as summer or spring break. You'll find a sample chart at the end of this chapter; or you can make your own chart and even vary the statements with each use so you can use it to start each day during the opening week of school.

Jog, Jump 'n Learn
Backwards Jeopardy

Purpose:
Assorted academics, brain-power-boosting brain break, readiness to focus & learn

Grades:
First through sixth grade

Duration:
One to five minutes – always keep them wanting more

Equipment Needed:
A list of two to five categories displayed on a SMART board, dry-erase board, flip chart…, one or more item(s) for each category kept in your head or on a handy list, music and music player OPTIONAL

How To:

1. List two to five categories on the board or flip chart. Have one or more items/answers that belong in / are for each category

2. Inform the kids that you are going to name people, places, and/or things and that each item you name belongs in one of the listed categories. Tell them that their job is to match what you say with one of the categories

3. Have the students jog in place continuously except for when they jump up with their answer (i.e., 3 jumps / repeat answer 3 times, once with each jump)

4. Let's say, for example, that the categories listed are: Mammal, Marsupial, Reptile & Amphibian. You say "frog" twice and give them time to think while jogging, then say, "GO!" They jump up, clap their hands high over their heads three times while saying, "Amphibian, amphibian, amphibian!" You tell them that if they said amphibian, they were correct. Possible other items to be categorized are: Cow, kangaroo, snake, lion alligator...The possible categories are endless from wars (History) to parts of speech (Language Arts) to angles (Geometry)...Try assigning differing numbers of jumps to different categories (e.g., for parts of speech you might include verbs 3 jumps, nouns 4, adjectives 5, adverbs 3).

This is a great activity for finding out what they know about an upcoming area of study, to find out if they are ready to move on to a new topic or to review for a quiz or test.

Tips:

Here are two options. You can ask the questions yourself and have a student lead the jogging and jumping; Or you can actively participate while a student leader states the items to be categorized. By picking a different student each time based on merit and promising that everyone who does a good job will eventually get a chance to be the leader, the youngsters will have more of an incentive to do their very best.

Optional: Put on some upbeat music that will energize the class.

Modify to meet your needs or the needs of individual students. For example, a student in a wheelchair can pump his arms like he's running and clap his hands overhead during the jumping action.

Backwards Jeopardy is a great way to start each science, math, social studies lesson and to use any time your youngsters need a break from seated activities. It really is as simple as jotting two to five categories on the board, having the kids stand up beside their desks and start listening, choosing and stating their answers while jogging and jumping. And the kids will love it and you for doing it!

Jog, Jump 'n Math

Purpose:
To learn & practice math facts, brain-power-boosting brain break, readiness to focus & learn

Grades:
First through fifth grades

Duration:
One to five minutes – always keep them wanting more

Equipment Needed:
Math flash cards with addition, subtraction, multiplication and/or division basic facts / equations on them

How To:
Have students jog-in-place beside their desks continuously throughout the *Jog, Jump 'n Math* session, except for the interludes of jumping. While they jog, display a math card with an equation on it minus the answer (e.g., 6 x 7 =). State the equation twice, the first time without the word "equals." The second time you say the equation add the word "equals." By stating the equation twice, you

are giving those who don't know or aren't sure time to think/figure out the answer. Right after you say the word "equals," they jump up three times quickly in succession. At the top of each jump they clap their hands overhead a single time and say the answer. For example, they jog while you say, "6 times 7, 6 times 7 EQUALS" and then they immediately jump up three times saying, "42, 42, 42!" Then turn the card over to show them the equation with the answer and say, "That's right, 7 x 6 = 42" or "If you said 42, you were correct."

If it sounds like everyone said, "42," put the card in the answered-right pile. On the other hand, if you hear some voices saying an answer that is not "42," then put the card in the need-to-learn pile. Repeat this process with the cards from the need-to-learn pile until there are no cards left in this grouping.

Tips:

Here are two options. You can display the cards and say the equations yourself while having a student to come to the front of the room and lead the jogging and jumping; or you can actively participate with the students and as the leader while a selected student holds up the cards and says the equations. By picking a different student each time based on merit and promising that everyone who does a good job will get a chance to be the leader eventually, the youngsters will have more of an incentive to do their very best.

The second time you say the problem/equation have the students say it in unison with you and end with their jumping up three times with the answer, as above.

Optional: Put on some upbeat music to energize the class.

Modify to meet your needs or the needs of individual students. For example, a student in a wheelchair can pump his arms like he's running and clap his hands overhead during the jumping action.

Jog, Jump 'n Math is a great way to start each math session and at any time your youngsters need a break from seated activities. It really is as simple as picking up a stack of math cards, having the kids stand up beside their desks, pushing the button on the music source and starting with the first card/equation. And the kids will love it and you for doing it!

Jog, Jump 'n Rhyme

Purpose:
To learn about rhyming, improve reading skills, understand & appreciate poetry, brain-power-boosting brain break, enhance readiness to focus & learn

Grades:
Preschool through fifth grade (pre-readers repeat rather than read)

Duration:
One to five minutes – always keep them wanting more

Equipment Needed:
A poem appropriate for the grade level and the equipment/materials needed to display it (with the rhyming words underlined, bolded or otherwise identified/marked)

How To:
Have students jog-in-place beside their desks continuously throughout the *Jog, Jump 'n Rhyme* session, except for the jumping interludes. While they are jogging have them read

the poem with you. When they get to the underlined or otherwise marked rhyming words, they jump up three times quickly in succession. At the top of each jump they clap their hands overhead a single time and say the rhyming word. Let's use *Little Miss Muffet* as our example:

Little Miss **Muffet**

Sat on a **tuffet**

Eating her curds and **whey**

Along came a **spider**

Who sat down **beside her**

And frightened Miss **Muffet away**

With this poem, when they get to the underlined word, "Muffet," they immediately jump up three times saying, "Muffet, Muffet, Muffet!" They continue in this fashion, jogging and then jumping up and saying the rhyming word every time they come to one. With shorter poems such as this example, you may want to repeat the poem two or more times.

A numbered list of the rhyming words in the poem can also be made. With *Little Miss Muffet* it might look like this:

1. **Muffet** rhymes with _____!

2. **Beside her** rhymes with _____!

3. **Whey** rhymes with _____!

4. **Spider** rhymes with _____ _____!

5. **Away** rhymes with _____!

For this numbered list of rhyming words, you say the number of the sentence you want them to read and they jump up and say the rhyming-underlined word 3 times, then jog while reading the NOT underlined words and finally, jump up 3 times while saying the fill-in-the-blank word that rhymes with the starting rhyming word (i.e. same as they did while reading the poem).

In addition, you can make up some questions related to the poem for them to answer. As with the poem and previously-described numbered list of rhyming words, have them jog-in-place while reading the sentence and then jump up three times while saying the answers. Here is an example of the types of *questions* you might ask / statements you might list:

1. The main character is _____!

2. Who sat down beside her? _____

3. What did Miss Muffet do? _____

4. What would you have done? _____

5. Something that frightens me is _____!

Tips:

Here are two options. You can point out each word in the poem to be read as it is being read by the class, while a student stands in front of the room leading the jogging and jumping; Or you can actively participate with the students and as the leader while a selected student points out the words to be read. By picking a different student each time based on merit and promising that everyone who does a good job will get a chance to eventually be the leader, the youngsters will have more of an incentive to do their very best.

Remember to encourage them to jump energetically/powerfully.

Modify to meet your needs or the needs of individual students. For example, a student who has just returned from being sick, can stay seated and pump his arms like he's running and clap his hands overhead during the jumping action.

Jog, Jump 'n Rhyme is a great way to start each language arts / reading session and any time your youngsters need a break from seated activities. It really is as simple as displaying one of several poems (with rhyming words designated/marked) that you have stored on your computer or on your giant flip chart, having the kids stand up beside their desks and start reading the poem while jogging, jumping and rhyming joyfully. And the kids will love it and you for doing it!

There is a chart for the Little Miss Muffet poem at the end of this chapter.

Jog, Jump 'n Parts of Speech

Purpose:
To learn about nouns, pronouns, verbs, subject, object, etc., improve reading skills, understand & appreciate good writing, brain-power-boosting brain break, enhance readiness to focus & learn

Grades:
Third through sixth grades (Primary grades for subject, verb, object)

Duration:
One to five minutes – always keep them wanting more

Equipment Needed:

Numbered sentences or other text with selected words under-lined or otherwise designated (e.g. all nouns and verbs under-lined) and the equipment/materials needed for the display of the sentences/text

How To:

Have students continuously jog in place beside their desks throughout the *Jog, Jump 'n Parts of Speech* session, except for the jumping interludes. While they are jogging, read the sentences/text to them while they follow along visually. When you read/say an underlined or otherwise marked word, they jump up three times quickly in succession. At the top of each jump they clap their hands overhead a single time and say the part of speech. Let's use this example:

1. The powerful **horse** on a beautiful **day** in **May jumped** over a very tall **fence**.

When you read the word "horse," they jump up three times and say, "Noun, noun, noun!" Skipping ahead, when you get to "jumped," they all jump up and state, "Verb, verb, verb!" Continue in this fashion. If the class identifies all the parts of speech in the sentence correctly, move on to the next sentence. If, however, you hear some wrong answers among the chorus of correct answers, then go back and repeat this sentence until you only hear correct answers. You might want the class to read the sentences/text in unison with you rather than just having you read to them.

Tips:

Here are two options. You can point out each word in the text/sentences as you read them to the class, while a student stands in front of the room leading the jogging and jumping; or you can actively participate with the students and as the leader while a selected student points out the words (as you or he read(s) them) to help direct their visual attention. By picking a different student each time based on merit and promising that everyone who does a good job will eventually get a chance to be the leader, the youngsters will have more of an incentive to do their very best.

Optional: Put on some upbeat music to energize the class.

Modify to meet your needs or the needs of individual students. For example, a student who has just returned from being sick, can participate while seated, pumping his arms like he's running and then clapping his hands overhead during the jumping action.

Jog, Jump 'n Parts of Speech is a great way to start each language arts / reading class and works well any time your youngsters need a break from seated activities. Besides nouns and verbs, you can do adverbs, adjectives, pronouns, subject, object, and other parts of speech, parts of sentences and even punctuation. It really is as simple as displaying sentences/texts (with selected words highlighted) that you have stored on your computer or on your giant flip chart and having the kids stand up beside their desks and start listening and following along visually while jogging, jumping and joyfully naming the parts of speech. And the kids will love it and you for doing it!

This OR That

Academic Version

Purpose:
To preview, review or learn science, social studies and other academic material, brain-power-boosting brain break, enhance readiness to focus & learn

Grades:
Kindergarten through sixth grade

Duration:
One to five minutes – always keep them wanting more

Equipment Needed:
Individual cards with two answers on each card (e.g., Saturn or Jupiter)

How To:
Have students continuously jog in place beside their desks throughout the *This OR That* session, except for the jumping interludes. While they are jogging hold up a card with two answers on it. Ask them a question to which one of the two words or phrases on the card is the correct answer. When you have finished saying the two choices, they jump up three times quickly in succession. At the top of each jump they clap their hands overhead a single time and say the answer. Let's use *Saturn OR Jupiter* as our example:

While they jog you ask, "Which is the largest planet in our solar system, Saturn or Jupiter?" Right after you say "Jupiter," they jump up three times quickly in succession and say, "Jupiter, Jupiter, Jupiter!" Another option is to give them time to think / figure it out by having them wait to jump until you say, "Go!"

If it sounds like everyone said, "Jupiter," put the card in the answered-right pile. On the other hand, if you hear some voices saying "Saturn," then put the card in the need-to-learn pile. Repeat this process with the cards from the need-to-learn pile until there are no cards left in this grouping.

This is a great activity for finding out what they know about an upcoming area of study, to find out if they are ready to move on to a new topic or to review for a quiz or test.

Tips:

Here are two options. You can display the cards and ask the questions yourself and have a student come to the front of the room and lead the jogging and jumping; or you can actively participate while asking the questions with a selected student holding the cards up. By picking a different student each time based on merit and promising that everyone who does a good job will eventually get a chance to be the leader, the youngsters will have more of an incentive to do their very best.

Optional: Put on some upbeat music to energize the class.

Modify to meet your needs or the needs of individual students. For example, a student in a wheelchair can pump his arms like he's running and clap his hands overhead during the jumping action.

This OR That is a great way to start each science, math, social studies, etc. lesson and works well any time your youngsters need a break from seated activities. It really is as simple as throwing together a set of cards, having the kids stand up beside their desks and start listening and following along visually while jogging, jumping and joyfully choosing their answers. And the kids will love it and you for doing it!

This OR That
Halloween Version

Purpose:
Reading/vocabulary, Halloween seasonal fun, brain-power-boosting brain break, enhance readiness to focus & learn

Grades:
Kindergarten through sixth grade

Duration:
One to five minutes – always keep them wanting more

Equipment Needed:
A numbered list of 10 to 20 Halloween-themed choices displayed on a SMART board, dry-erase board, flip chart...For Example:

1. Skeleton OR Ghost

2. Frankenstein's Monster OR Dracula

3. Mask OR Face Painted

Note: Halloween chart supplied at the end of chapter.

How To:
Have students continuously jog in place beside their desks throughout the Halloween-themed *This OR That* session, except for the jumping interludes. While they are jogging, say, for example, "Number one -- would you rather see a skeleton or a ghost?" When you have told them the two choices, they jump up three times quickly in succession. At the top

of each jump they clap their hands overhead a single time and say their choice. Let's use 3. Mask OR Face Painted as another example.

You might say, "Would you rather wear a mask or have your face painted?" When you have read both choices to them, they jump up three times and say, "Mask, mask, mask!" or "Face paint, face paint, face paint!" Continue in this fashion through the list of choices.

Tips:

Here are two options. You can point out each word as you read it to the class, while a student stands in front of the room leading the jogging and jumping; or you can actively participate with the students while reading the words to them, while, to help direct their visual attention, a student leader points at the words. To keep them even more visually attentive, you can state the choices out of numerical order.

By picking a different student each time based on merit and promising that everyone who does a good job will eventually get a chance to be the leader, the youngsters will have more of an incentive to do their very best.

Optional: Put on some upbeat and spooky / Halloween-themed music to energize and more fully engage the class.

Modify to meet your needs or the needs of individual students. For example, a student who has just returned from being sick, can stay seated and pump his arms like he's running and clap his hands overhead during the jumping action.

A Halloween-Themed *This OR That* session *is* a great way to start a reading class or to use when your youngsters need a break from seated activities during the month of October. Use the chart at the end of this chapter or make up your own list of Halloween choices. It really is as simple as displaying my list or your own of Halloween-themed choices, having the kids stand up beside their desks and start to listen and follow along visually while jogging, jumping and joyfully exclaiming their choices. And the kids will love it and you for doing it!

Jog, Jump 'n Thanksgiving

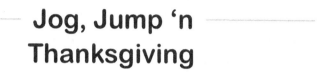

Purpose:
To practice reading & learn vocabulary, for seasonal fun, to promote feelings of appreciation, brain-power-boosting brain break, enhance readiness to focus & learn

Grades:
Kindergarten to sixth grade and up, depending on the youngster(s) or group (e.g. groups of adults greatly enjoy this, too) – not a reading activity for youngest

Duration:
One to five minutes – always keep them wanting more

Equipment Needed:
A numbered list of 10 to 20 open-ended statements displayed on a SMART board, dry-erase board, flip chart...For Example:

1. A food I give thanks for IS _____!

2. Someone I am thankful for IS _____!

3. I give thanks for being able TO _____!

Note: Thanksgiving-themed chart supplied at the end of this chapter.

How To:

Have students jog in place beside their desks continuously throughout the *Jog, Jump 'n Thanksgiving* session, except for the jumping interludes. While they jog, have them read (or repeat after you) the statements out loud and in unison. Right after they say the last word before the fill-in-the-blank, they jump up three times quickly in succession. At the top of each jump, they clap their hands overhead a single time and say their unique answer. For example, they jog while reading/saying, "I give thanks for being able TO" and then immediately jump up three times saying, "Tie my shoes, tie my shoes, tie my shoes!" OR "Ride a bike, ride a bike, ride a bike!" OR...

Tips:

Before starting, go over any words or statements with which you think the class might have trouble. Actively participate as the leader for the class or pick a student leader. While a student is leading the jogging and jumping, you can point to each word as it is being read. Also, to even more fully engage them visually, pick the statements out of numerical order.

Optional: Put on some upbeat music to energize the class. Follow up this activity with a discussion of their favorite answers and/or write or draw a picture about that for which they are most thankful.

Modify to meet your needs or the needs of individual students. For example, a student in a wheelchair can pump her arms like she's running and clap her hands overhead during the jumping action.

Jog, Jump 'n Thanksgiving is the perfect November activity. Use it to start reading class or when your youngsters need a break from seated activities during this time of year when we are reminded to be thankful for all our blessings.

This OR That
Christmas/Winter Version

Purpose:
Reading/vocabulary, Christmas/winter-season fun, brain-power-boosting brain break, enhance readiness to focus & learn

Grades:
Kindergarten through sixth grade

Duration:
One to five minutes – always keep them wanting more

Equipment Needed:
A numbered list of 10 to 20 Christmas/Winter-themed choices displayed on a SMART board, dry-erase board, flip chart...For Example:

1. Build a snowman OR go sledding
2. Rudolph OR Frosty

Note: Christmas/Winter-Themed chart supplied at end of chapter.

How To:
Have students continuously jog in place beside their desks throughout the Christmas/Winter-Themed *This OR That* session, except for the jumping interludes. While they are jogging, say, for example, "Number one -- would you rather build a snowman or go sledding?" When you have told them the two choices, they jump up three times quickly in succession. At the top of each jump, they clap their hands overhead

a single time and say their choice. More specifically, when you have read both choices to them, they jump up three times and say, "Build a snowman, build a snowman, build a snowman!" or "Go sledding, go sledding, go sledding!" Continue in this fashion through the list of choices.

Tips:

Here are two options. You can point out each word/phrase as you read them to the class, while a student stands in front of the room leading the jogging and jumping; or you can actively participate with the students and as the leader of the activity while a selected student points out the words as you read them to help direct their visual attention. To keep them more visually attentive, you can also state the choices out of numerical order.

By picking a different student each time based on merit and promising that everyone who does a good job will eventually get a chance to be the leader, the youngsters will have more of an incentive to do their very best.

Optional: Put on some upbeat Christmas/Winter-themed music to energize and more fully engage the class.

Modify to meet your needs or the needs of individual students. For example, a student who has just returned from being sick can stay seated and pump his arms like he's running and clap his hands overhead during the jumping action.

A Christmas/Winter-themed *This OR That* session *is* a great way to start reading class or to use when your youngsters need a break from seated activities during the month of December. Use the chart at the end of this chapter or make up your own list of Christmas/Winter choices. It really is as simple as displaying my list or your own of these seasonal-themed choices, having the kids stand up beside their desks and start listening and following along visually while jogging, and then jumping while joyfully exclaiming their choices. And the kids will love it and you for doing it!

Jog, Jump 'n Learn

New Year's Edition

Purpose:
Reading/vocabulary, spirit-lifting / brain-power-boosting brain break, enhance readiness to focus & learn

Grades:
Preschool to fifth grade and up depending on the youngster(s) or group (e.g. groups of adults greatly enjoy this, too) – not a reading activity for youngest

Duration:
One to five minutes – always keep them wanting more

Equipment Needed:
A numbered list of 10 to 20 open-ended statements displayed on a SMART board, dry-erase board, flip chart...For Example:

1. In the year 20 _ _ a game I want to play IS _____!

2. This year I want to learn how TO _____!

Note: New Year's edition chart supplied at end of chapter.

How To:
Have students continuously jog in place beside their desks throughout the New Year's edition of a *Jog, Jump 'n Learn* session, interrupted only by the jumping interludes. While

they are jogging, say, for example, "Number one -- In the year 20 _ _ a game I want to play IS _____!" Right after the word "IS" is read, they jump up three times quickly in succession. At the top of each jump they clap their hands overhead a single time and say their unique answer. For this example, on the word "IS," they jump up three times and say, "Tag, tag, tag!" or "Checkers, checkers, checkers!" or "___, ___, ___!" Continue in this fashion through the list of open-ended statements.

Tips:

Here are two options. You can point out each word as you and the class read them in unison, while a student stands in front of the room leading the jogging and jumping; Or you can actively participate with the students as the leader of the activity while a selected student points out the words (to help direct their visual attention) and as you and the class read them. To keep them even more visually attentive and focused, you can do the open-ended statements out of numerical order.

By picking a different student each time, based on merit and promising that everyone who does a good job will eventually get a chance to be the leader, the youngsters will have more of an incentive to do their very best.

Optional: Put on some upbeat music to energize the class.

Modify to meet your needs or the needs of individual students. For example, a student who has just returned from being sick, can stay seated and pump his arms like he's running and clap his hands overhead during the jumping action.

A New Year's-themed *Jog, Jump 'n Learn* session *is* a great way to start back from winter break or to start reading class or when the class needs a break from extended sitting. Use the chart at the end of this chapter or make up your own list of New Year's exclamations. It really is as simple as displaying my (or your own) list of these seasonal-themed statements, having the kids stand up beside their desks and start following along by listening and reading while jogging, and then jumping up and joyfully exclaiming their personal preferences. The kids will love it and you for doing it!

Jog, Jump 'n Learn
February / Valentine's Day

Purpose:
Reading/ vocabulary, spirit-lifting Valentine's Day-themed fun, brain-power-boosting brain break, enhance readiness to focus & learn

Grades:
Kindergarten through sixth grade

Duration:
One to five minutes – always keep them wanting more

Equipment Needed:
A numbered list of 10 to 20 Valentine's Day-themed open-ended statements or This-or-That choices displayed on a SMART board, dry-erase board, flip chart...For Example:

1. A place I LOVE to visit IS _____!
2. Which do you LOVE or LIKE more: Valentine's Day party OR a birthday party

Note: A Valentine's Day themed chart is supplied at the end of this chapter.

How To:

Have students continuously jog in place beside their desks throughout the Valentine's Day-Themed *Jog, Jump 'n Learn* session, except for the jumping interludes. While they are jogging, say, for example, "Number two -- would you rather go to a Valentine's Day party or a birthday party?" When you have told them the two choices, they jump up three times quickly in succession. At the top of each jump they clap their hands overhead a single time and say their choice. In this example, when you have read both choices to them, they jump up three times and say, "Valentine's Day party, Valentine's Day party, Valentine's Day party!" or "birthday party, birthday party, birthday party!" Continue in this fashion through the list of choices.

For the open-ended statements, right after the word "IS" is read, they jump up three times quickly in succession. At the top of each jump they clap their hands overhead a single time and say their unique answer. For example, in answer to *1. A place I LOVE to visit*, they might jump up three times and say, "The beach, the beach, the beach!" or "Grandma's house, Grandma's house, Grandma's house!" or " _____, _____, _____!"

Tips:

Here are two options. You can point out each word/phrase as you read it to the class, while a student stands in front of the room leading the jogging and jumping; or you can actively participate with the students and, as the leader of the activity, while a selected student points out the words (to help direct their visual attention) as you read the words to them. To keep them more visually attentive, you can state the choices out of numerical order.

By picking a different student each time based on merit and promising that everyone who does a good job will eventually get a chance to be the leader, the youngsters will have more of an incentive to do their very best.

Optional: Put on some upbeat Valentine's Day-themed music to energize the class and set the mood.

Modify to meet your needs or the needs of individual students. For example, a student who has just returned from being sick can stay seated and pump his arms like he's running and clap his hands overhead during the jumping action.

A Valentine's Day *Jog, Jump 'n Learn* session *is* a great way to start reading class or to use whenever your young-sters need a break from seated activities during the month of February. Use the chart at the end of this chapter or make up your own list of Valentine's Day-themed choices or open-ended statements. It really is as simple as displaying my list (or your own) of these seasonal-themed choices; have the kids stand up beside their desks and start listening and fol-lowing along visually / reading in unison while jogging, and then jumping up and joyfully exclaiming their choices. AND, the kids will love it and you for doing it!

This OR That

Spring/Summer/End-of-Year Version

Purpose:
Reading/vocabulary, spirit-lifting spring/summer and end-of-year-fun, brain-power-boosting brain break, enhance readiness to focus & learn

Grades:
Kindergarten through sixth grade

Duration:
One to five minutes – always keep them wanting more

Equipment Needed:
A numbered list of 10 to 20 spring/summer-themed choices displayed on a SMART board, dry-erase board, flip chart... For Example:

1. Swimming pool OR the beach

2. Game of tag OR Computer game

How To:
Have students continuously jog in place beside their desks throughout the Spring/Summer-Themed *This OR That* session, except for the jumping interludes. While they are jogging, say, for example, "Number three -- would you rather go to a swimming pool or the beach?" When you have told them the two choices, they jump up three times quickly in succession. At the top of each jump they clap their hands overhead a single time and say their choice. In this example, when you have read both choices to them, they jump up three times and say, "Swimming pool, swimming pool, swimming pool!" or "The beach, the beach, the beach!" Continue in this fashion through the list of choices.

Tips:
Here are two options. You can point out each word/phrase as you and they read them out loud in unison, while a student stands in front of the room leading the jogging and jumping; or you can actively participate with the students while a student leader points out the words (to help direct their visual attention) as you and the class read them. To

keep them even more visually engaged, the choices can be presented out of numerical order.

By picking a different student each time based on merit and promising that everyone who does a good job will eventually get a chance to be the leader, the youngsters will have more of an incentive to do their very best.

Optional: Put on some upbeat, spring/summer-themed music to energize and better engage the class.

Modify to meet your needs or the needs of individual students. For example, a student who has just returned from being sick, can stay seated and pump his arms like he's running and clap his hands overhead during the jumping action.

A Spring/Summer-Themed *This OR That* session *is* a great way to start reading class or to use whenever your youngsters need a break from seated activities during the spring. Use the chart at the end of this chapter or make up your own list of spring/summer choices. It really is as simple as displaying my list or your own of these seasonal-themed choices, having the kids stand up beside their desks and listening and following along visually while jogging, and then jumping up and joyfully exclaiming their choices. AND, the kids will love it and you for doing it!

This OR That

Jump for Joy

Purpose:
Reading/vocabulary, spirit-lifting / brain-power-boosting brain break, enhance readiness to focus & learn

Grades:
Kindergarten through sixth grade

Duration:
One to five minutes – always keep them wanting more

Equipment Needed:
A numbered list of 10 to 20 fun choices displayed on a SMART board, dry-erase board, flip chart...For Example:

1. Drawing OR Singing
2. Playground OR Computer Lab

How To:
Have students continuously jog in place beside their desks throughout the Jump for Joy version of the *This OR That* session, interrupted only by the jumping interludes. While they are jogging, say, for example, "Number one -- would you rather enjoy drawing pictures or singing songs?" When you have told them the two choices, they jump up three times quickly in succession. At the top of each jump they clap their hands overhead a single time and say their choice. In this example, when you have read both choices to them, they jump up three times and say, "Drawing, drawing, drawing!" or "Singing, singing, singing!" Continue in this fashion through the list of choices.

Tips:
Here are two options. You can point out each word/phrase as you read them to the class, while a student stands in front of the room leading the jogging and jumping; or you can actively participate with the students and as the leader of the activity while a selected student points out the words to help direct their visual attention as you read to them. To keep them even more visually attentive, you can state the

choices out of numerical order.

By picking a different student each time based on merit and promising that everyone who does a good job will eventually get a chance to be the leader, the youngsters will have more of an incentive to do their very best.

Optional: Put on some upbeat music to energize and better engage the class.

Modify to meet your needs or the needs of individual students. For example, a student who has just returned from being sick can stay seated and pump his arms like he's running and clap his hands overhead during the jumping action.

This brain break / *This OR That* session *is* a great way to start reading class or to use whenever your youngsters need a break from seated activities. Use the chart at the end of this chapter or make up your own list of Jump for Joy choices. It really is as simple as displaying my list, or your own, of these fun choices, having the kids stand up beside their desks and start listening and following along visually while jogging, and then jumping up and joyfully exclaiming their choices. The kids will love it and you for doing it!

Find Brain Sprints videos at:
YouTube.com, enter "Brain Sprints Math"
or "Ed Mayhew Brain Sprints" or visit
SmarterStrongerChildren.com

Jog, Jump 'n Learn and This OR That Charts

The following charts will help you boost the brain power of your youngsters. They can be used in these ways:

1. Place them as is under your camera/Elmo to display them on your Smart Board. Enlarge the magnification so the students can read them while running and jumping beside their desks.

2. Copy them onto a giant flip chart or dry-erase board.

3. Use them to stimulate ideas for creating your own personal versions of the *This OR That* and *Jog, Jump 'n Learn* charts.

Remember that these aren't just cute little activities / brain breaks. With regular use, they actually significantly improve the structure and function of your children's brains! They are fun for the students, but they are also very powerful *tools* for learning.

Jump for Joy

Great Start to New Schoolyear, Week ...

1. A food I like to eat IS ____!
2. My favorite drink IS ____!
3. A toy I like to play with IS ____!
4. A game I really enjoy playing IS ____!
5. When outdoors something I like to do IS ____!
6. When indoors one of the things I like to do IS ____!
7. A cartoon I like to watch IS ____!
8. A person I like to be with IS ____!
9. A meal I look forward to IS ____!
10. A place I like to go IS ____!
11. Something I'm proud I can do IS ____!
12. A sport I enjoy playing IS ____!
13. The very coolest animal IS ____!
14. I am happiest WHEN ____!
15. What I would like to do someday IS ___!
16. My very favorite holiday IS ____!
17. A school subject I like IS ____!
18. I am happy when I get TO ____!
19. I would like to have the money TO ____!
20. The one wish I would like to come true IS ____!

Jog, Jump 'n Learn

Addition & Subtraction
Family of Facts: 2,7,9; 3,6,9; 4,5,9

A. $7 + 2 = 9$ G. $9 - 3 = 6$

B. $2 + 7 = 9$ H. $9 - 6 = 3$

C. $9 - 2 = 7$ I. $5 + 4 = 9$

D. $9 - 7 = 2$ J. $4 + 5 = 9$

E. $6 + 3 = 9$ K. $9 - 4 = 5$

F. $3 + 6 = 9$ L. $9 - 5 = 4$

Instructions: Display this chart, put on some lively music and instruct students to jog in place, beside their desks, continuously except for when jumping up with the answer. Direct their attention to equation A and say, "7 + 2." Then say the equation a 2nd time with them saying it with you and adding the equal sign. Immediately after saying, "equals," they jump up 3 times quickly in succession; at the top of each jump they clap their hands overhead and say the answer a single time (i.e. they say each answer 3 times – once with each of the 3 jumps. Continue in this fashion through the whole list of the equations / families of facts. Optional: Cover the answers with a strip of paper and slide the strip down one equation after each set of 3 jumps/3 answers so students can check their answers. **Flash cards can be used in place of the list.**

Jump, Jog 'n Rhyme

Little Miss Muffet

Little Miss <u>Muffet</u>

Sat on a <u>tuffet</u>

Eating her curds and <u>whey</u>

Along came a <u>spider</u>

Who sat down <u>beside her</u>

And frightened Miss <u>Muffet away</u>

1. <u>Muffet</u> rhymes with _____!

2. <u>Beside her</u> rhymes with _____!

3. <u>Whey</u> rhymes with _____!

4. <u>Spider</u> rhymes with _____ _____!

5. <u>Away</u> rhymes with _____!

Jog, Jump 'n Read & Comprehend

Little Miss Muffet

Little Miss Muffet

Sat on a tuffet

Eating her curds and whey

Along came a spider

Who sat down beside her

And frightened Miss Muffet away

Directions: Jog 'n read and then jump up 3 times with the answer to each of these 5 questions.

1. The main character is _____

2. Who sat down beside her? _____

3. What did Miss Muffet do? _____

4. What would you have done? _____

5. Something that frightens me is _____

Jog, Jump 'n Rhyme

Brain Sprints Are Great

Brain Sprints, Brain Sprints - Good for head and **HEART**

Brain Sprints, Brain Sprints - Make me really **SMART**

Brain Sprints, Brain Sprints – Get me up to **RUN**

Brain Sprints, Brain Sprints – Good for EVERY**ONE**

Brain Sprints, Brain Sprints – Makes me really **FAST**

Brain Sprints, Brain Sprints – They're a total **BLAST**

Brain Sprints, Brain Sprints – Help me ace the **TEST**

Brain Sprints, Brain Sprints – Are the very **BEST**

Brain Sprints, Brain Sprints - Make learning lots of **FUN**

Brain Sprints, Brain Sprints - Clearly number **ONE**

Brain Sprints, Brain Sprints - How do they **RATE?**

Brain Sprints, Brain Sprints - They rate – super **GREAT!**

Instructions: Students jog-in-place as teacher and students read the poem in unison. When they come to a rhyming/bolded word, the students jump up three times (clapping hands one-time, high overhead at top of each jump) saying the rhyming word three times, i.e. saying the word once at the top of each jump. Encourage energetic jumps and easy jogging. Repeat two or three times and have fun with this. Best when the teacher participates in the jogging and jumping or chooses a student to lead the class. © Ed Mayhew, creator of the Brain Sprints / Mega Brain-Power Boosters program. SmarterStrongerChildren.com

This OR That

Academics Version -- Astronomy

1. Our solar system – 8 OR 10 Planets

2. Orbits Earth – Sun OR Moon

3. Sun is – Large Moon OR Medium Star

4. Closest to Sun – Mercury OR Venus

5. Furthest out – Saturn OR Neptune

6. Stars are Smaller OR Larger than Earth

7. Largest planet – Jupiter OR Saturn

8. Known for its rings – Saturn OR Mars

9. Stars are mostly – Gas OR Rock

10. Our atmosphere mostly Oxygen OR Hydrogen

11. Closest star 1,000 OR 23 Trillion miles

12. Our Galaxy – Andromeda OR Milky Way

13. Our Galaxy – 100 OR 100 Billion stars

14. Earth orbits Sun – 30 days OR 365 days

15. Moon called – Meteor OR Satellite

16. Moon closer to – Earth OR Sun

17. Number Galaxies – 200 OR 200 Billion

18. Space between planets – Heliosphere OR Atmosphere

19. Dwarf Planet – Gemini OR Pluto

20. Study of Universe – Astronomy OR Astrology

This OR That

Halloween Version

1. Skeleton OR Ghost
2. Frankenstein's Monster OR Dracula
3. Spooky OR Really Scary
4. Black Bat OR Black Cat
5. Witch OR Princess
6. Count Dracula OR Zombie
7. Pirate OR Cowboy/Cowgirl
8. Candy Corn OR Candy Bar
9. Wax Teeth OR Fake Blood
10. Mask OR Face Paint
11. Superman OR Batman
12. Wonder Woman OR Supergirl
13. Scary Movie OR Cartoon
14. Haunted House OR Graveyard
15. Cute Jack-o-lantern OR Scary One
16. Trick or Treat OR Halloween Party
17. Party Games OR Party Food
18. Graveyard at Night OR Giant Spider
19. Carve Pumpkin OR Dress Up
20. Halloween Night OR Fireworks Display

Jump, Jog 'n Thanksgiving

1. Someone I am thankful for IS ____!

2. A place I give thanks for IS ____!

3. A toy I am thankful for IS ____!

4. A game I give thanks for IS ____!

5. A sport I am thankful for IS ____!

6. A book I give thanks for IS ____!

7. A cartoon I am thankful for IS ____!

8. A meal I give thanks for IS ____!

9. A Dessert I am thankful for IS ____!

10. A drink I give thanks for IS ____!

11. I am thankful that I CAN ____!

12. I give thanks that I can MAKE ____!

13. I am thankful that I AM ____!

14. I give thanks that I am GOOD AT ____!

15. A school subject I give thanks for IS ___!

16. I am thankful I can be helpful BY ____!

17. I give thanks that I HAVE ____!

18. I am thankful when I get TO ____!

19. I give thanks I can take care OF ____!

20. The greatest thing I am thankful for IS ____!

Ed Mayhew

This OR That

Christmas/Winter Version

1. Build a Snowman OR Go Sledding
2. Song: Jingle Bells OR Rudolph
3. Snow OR Sunshine
4. Elf on a Shelf OR Santa Claus
5. Green OR Red
6. Frosty OR Frozen's Olaf
7. Reindeer OR Ponies
8. Snowmobile OR Sleigh Ride
9. Play in Snow OR on Computer
10. Ebenezer Scrooge OR The Grinch
11. Doll/Action Figure OR Another Toy
12. Hot Chocolate OR Eggnog
13. Decorating OR Wrapping Gifts
14. Shovel Snow OR Clean Room
15. Bedtime Story OR One More TV Show
16. Art Project OR Shopping
17. Holiday Lights OR Holiday Sounds
18. Give Gift OR Receive Gift
19. Angels in Snow OR Snowball Fight
20. Know What Getting OR Be Surprised

Jump, Jog 'n Learn

New Year's Edition

1. In the year 20 _ _ a game I want to play IS ____!

2. This year I want to learn how TO ____!

3. Someone I would like to spend more time with this year IS ____!

4. A food I want to eat more often this year IS ____!

5. When it snows this year I want TO ____!

6. When it is hot this summer I look forward TO ____!

7. A cartoon I wish to watch often IS ____!

8. In 20 _ _ I will be helpful BY ____!

9. A place I want to visit this year IS ____!

10. Something I plan on doing this year IS _

11. A sport I can play this year IS ____!

12. Something I can make this year IS ____!

13. I am excited about learning how TO ____!

14. This year on my birthday I will BE ____!

15. I want others to know that I AM __!

16. The holiday I'm looking forward to IS ____!

17. When at home I look forward TO ____!

18. This is going to be a great year BECAUSE ____!

Valentine's Day/ February

1. A food I LOVE IS ____!

2. Something I LIKE to drink IS ____!

3. A person I LIKE a lot IS ____!

4. A book or story I LIKE IS ____!

5. A school subject I really LIKE IS ____!

6. A place I LOVE to visit IS ____!

7. A game I LIKE to play IS ____!

8. Something I would LOVE to do IS ____!

9. A sport's team or sport I LIKE IS ____!

10. Something I'd LOVE to have IS ____!

Which Do You LIKE or LOVE More?

1. Cartoons OR Movies
2. Playing Video Games OR Playing Tag
3. Math OR Reading
4. Pizza OR Ice Cream
5. Halloween OR Valentine's Day
6. Gym Class OR Art
7. Indoor Activities OR Outdoor Play
8. Swimming OR Playing in the Snow
9. School Days OR Weekends
10. Hugs OR High-Fives

This OR That
Spring/Summer-Themed Version

1. Swimming Pool OR The Beach
2. Game of Tag OR Computer Game
3. Art Project OR Ball Game
4. Carnival Rides OR Carnival Games
5. Candy Apple OR Cotton Candy
6. Ferris Wheel OR Merry-go-Round
7. Movie Theater Movie OR Carnival
8. July 4th – Parade OR Fireworks
9. Run Under Sprinkler OR Favorite Video
10. Lemonade OR Soda Pop
11. Corn on the Cob OR Watermelon
12. Cookout OR McDonalds
13. Hotdog OR Hamburger
14. Shoot Baskets or Play Catch
15. Football OR Soccer
16. Favorite Book OR TV Show
17. Bike Ride OR Playground Fun
18. Pizza Party OR Swimming Party
19. Water Park OR Themed Park
20. Bounce House OR Bowling

Instructions: Students jog-in-place as teacher reads two choices. As soon as both choices have been stated, the students jump up three times (clapping hands one-time, high overhead at top of each jump) saying their choice three times, i.e. once at the top of each jump. Encourage energetic jumps and easy jogging. Spirited music can motivate students. Your own "choices" can be substituted for these. © Ed Mayhew, creator of the Brain Sprints / Mega Brain-Power Boosters program. SmarterStrongerChildren.com

This OR That

Jump for Joy Version

1. Birthday Party OR Birthday Gifts

2. Ride Your Bike OR Shoot Baskets

3. Cake OR Cookies

4. Spinach OR Carrots

5. Pizza Party OR Swimming Party

6. Make a New Friend OR Alone Time

7. Get Driver's License OR on Ball Team

8. Play Inside OR Play Outside

9. Vacation: At Beach OR Theme Park

10. Art Project OR Ball Game

11. New Clothes/Outfit OR New Sneakers

12. Learn Guitar OR Learn Magic Tricks

13. Zoo OR Carnival

14. Favorite Movie or Favorite Cartoon

15. Learn to Juggle OR Learn a Dance

16. Tell a Joke OR Sing a Song

17. Look Great OR Feel Great

18. Play on a Team OR Play in a Band

19. Read a Book OR Do Math

20. Healthy & Happy OR Rich & Famous

Ed Mayhew

This OR That

Jump for Joy – Brain Break Version

1. Drawing Pictures OR Singing Songs
2. High Fives OR Hugs
3. Cereal OR Pancakes
4. Mickey Mouse OR Sponge Bob
5. Physical Education OR Computer Lab
6. Popsicle OR Ice Cream
7. Basketball OR Baseball
8. Math Class OR Reading Class
9. Computer Game OR Table Game
10. Ironman OR Superman
11. Miniature Golf OR Bowling
12. Pizza OR Family Cookout
13. Legos OR Action Figures / Dolls
14. Television OR Computer/Tablet
15. Pet Dog OR Pet Cat
16. Cartoon OR Movie
17. Lemonade Stand OR Shovel Snow
18. Monkeys OR Elephants
19. Guitar OR Drums
20. Win a Game OR Make a New Friend

CHAPTER TWO

Brain Sprints

10 minutes of HIIT (High Intensity Interval Training) gives the equivalent benefits of 45 minutes of moderate-intensity steady-state cardio — Study findings of researcher Martin Gibala and associates, 2016. **Brain Sprints** *are HIIT for the classroom & home.*

The brain-power-boosting activities in this book were originally collectively called the *Mega Brain-Power Boosters Program for Excellence* and the **Brain Sprints** were just one of many brain-power-boosting activities in the program. Now Brain Sprints refers to either the whole collection of brain-power boosters or the individual activities included in this chapter and the context will tell you which.

The Brain Sprints in this chapter are a form of High Intensity Interval Training (HIIT). HIIT sessions usually alternate short bursts of very intense exercise with longer periods of recovery (for Brain Sprints recovery is accomplished with moderate to light exercise). University studies at McMaster University in Canada and the University of Loughborough in

England, among others, have found that subjects following an HIIT protocol get similar results to that of those performing longer-sessions of continuous moderate aerobic exercise, but in one-third to one-fifth the time. That means that when your youngsters do a mere 5-minute Brain Sprints session with sufficient intensity, they have exercised the equivalent of jogging around the gym or playground for 15 to 25 minutes. The Brain Sprints presented here are extremely potent brain-power boosters and overall-well-being enhancers!

Brain Sprints are best utilized similarly to the way warm-ups are used by athletes. They are best placed at the beginning of a math or reading class, for example. We can think of them as lubrication for the brain. The Brain Sprints should not be combined with difficult problem solving and higher-order thinking activities. Brain Sprints limber up the brain, so to speak, for the more advanced thinking skills, such as better reading comprehension and math problem solving, in the minutes that follow them.

A 2-minute Brain Sprints Promo video can be found at SmarterStrongerChildren.com or on Youtube.com "Brain Sprints Math."

Brain Sprints

101 or Basic Jogging & Sprinting Version

Purpose:
Reading/spelling or basic math facts, brain-power-boosting brain break, readiness to focus & learn

Grades:
First to fifth grade and up, depending on the youngster(s) or group

Duration:
One to seven minutes – start with one or two minutes and increase duration as ready for it – always keep them wanting more

Equipment Needed:
A numbered list of words or a lettered list of basic math facts displayed on a SMART board, dry-erase board, flip chart..., (music and music player optional) For Example:

1. House

2. Horse

OR

A. $1 \times 3 = 3$
B. $2 \times 3 = 6$

How To:
Have students jog in place beside their desks. While they are jogging have them say and spell each word with you. If practicing basic math facts, have them state the equation with you while jogging.

SPELLING WORDS: State the word's number (to help students find the word and visually focus on the word), then say the word with them; next, spell the word and finally say, "spells ___." Repeat three times because we learn by repetition. For example: "Number One, House...H-o-u-s-e spells house; House...h-o-u-s-e spells house; House...h-o-u-s-e spells house. Number two, Horse...H-o-r-s-e spells horse; Horse...H-o-r-s-e spells horse; Horse...H-o-r-s-e spells horse." During each jogging segment tackle three words in this fashion.

Right after they've spelled the three words three times each, have them sprint in place right beside their desks for 15 to 30 seconds. Instruct and encourage them to lift knees about waist high with each step and to go as fast as they can for maximum benefit. While they are sprinting, point to a word for them to say/read. Have them repeat each word three to five or so times (to help cement it into their memories) before moving on to the next word. During the sprinting choose the words out of sequence and challenge them to see if they can be the first one to see and say the word at which you are pointing.

Optional: Have them see if they can be the first person to say three times the next word you point to (e.g., You point to the word "House" and they say as fast as they can, "House, house, house").

After the 15 to 30 seconds of sprinting, have them return to jogging and spelling the next set of three words (e.g., words 4, 5 and 6), as before. Then return to the sprinting and saying the words. Start off by limiting Brain Sprints sessions to one or two minutes and gradually, as they are ready, increase the number of words spelled per session until they can handle six or seven-minute sessions.

BASIC MATH FACTS (addition, subtraction, multiplication or division): Follow the same steps as used for the spelling of words. That is, while they are jogging, have them say each equation three times in unison before moving on to the next equation. When they have completed three equations (i.e., equations A., B. and C.) three times each, they switch to sprinting.

While they are sprinting, point to an equation for them to state. Give them time to repeat each equation two or more times before moving on to the next math fact. Choose the equations out of sequence and challenge them to see if they can be the first one to see and say the math fact at which you are pointing.

After the 15 to 30 seconds of sprinting, have them return to jogging and working on equations D, E and F, as before. Then return to the sprinting challenge. Start off by limiting Brain Sprints sessions to one or two minutes and gradually, as they are ready, increase until they can handle six- or seven-minute sessions.

Tips:

Here are two options. You can point out each word or equation as you state/spell them with the class, while a student stands in front of the room leading the jogging and sprinting; or you can actively participate with the students as the leader of the jogging and sprinting, while a selected student points out the words or equations to help direct their visual attention as you and the class read/state/spell them. To keep them even more visually attentive, you can state the choices out of numerical/alphabetical order. Another option instead of pointing to the words and equations, is to simply call out the letter of the math fact to be practiced or the number of the word to be spelled.

By picking a different student each time based on merit and promising that everyone who does a good job will eventually get a chance to be the leader, the youngsters will have more of an incentive to do their very best.

In the place of spelling words, maybe create a list of words with their definitions and an example sentence of their use. Instead of spelling the word, they state the definition and/or use the word in a sentence (in unison) while jogging and then say the word repeatedly while sprinting.

Optional: Put on some upbeat music to energize and better engage the class.

Modify to meet your needs or the needs of individual students. For example, a student who has just returned from being sick can stay seated and pump his arms like he's jogging or sprinting.

These Brain Breaks *are* a great way to start reading or math class or to use whenever your youngsters need a break from seated activities. Use the charts at the end of this chapter or make up your own list of spelling words or equations. It really is as simple as displaying my list or your own, having the kids stand up beside their desks to start listening/stating and follow along visually while jogging, and then sprinting and then REPEATING. The kids will love the Brain Sprints and you for letting them do them!

Brain Sprints
2.0 / Supercharged Version

Purpose:
Reading/spelling or basic math facts, brain-power-boosting brain break, readiness to focus & learn

Grades:
First to fifth grade and up depending on the youngster(s) or group

Duration:
One to seven minutes – start with one or two minutes and increase time as ready for it – always keep them wanting more

Equipment Needed:
A numbered list of words or a lettered list of basic math facts displayed on a SMART board, dry-erase board, flip chart..., OPTIONAL: music and music player, stickers or masking tape

How To:

There are only two differences between the Brain Sprints 101 and the 2.0 version. First, during the "jogging" portion, the cross-lateral *Supercharger* replaces the jogging. The other change involves the sprinting. Let's handle the sprinting difference first.

In this Brain Sprints 2.0, while they are sprinting in place, you'll name a letter designating one of the equations. The students are challenged to see how fast they can repeat the designated equation THREE TIMES. For example, for **B. 2 + 1 = 3** they would say, "2 + 1 = 3; 2 + 1 = 3; 2 + 1 = 3" as fast as they can. They then listen for you to say the next equation-designating letter, maybe "D." TIP: Do not acknowledge who finishes first; instead, quickly move on to the next/another equation or back to the *Supercharger* portion. This avoids arguments over who won. *The sprinting should only last for 20 to 30 seconds.*

The Supercharger

The advantage of the *Supercharger* over the jogging is that it is a cross-lateral activity that better improves communication and cooperation between the brain hemispheres. It does this by increasing the myelination of the axons of the *corpus callosum* (the 'bridge' connecting the hemispheres to one another). This is important because the hemispheres are specialists. The left hemisphere, for instance, is usually used for basic math facts, while the right tends to be more for advanced math problem solving.

The downside of using the *Supercharger* is that a good number of children, especially younger ones ages seven and younger, can't perform this relatively simple cross-lateral movement. They have to be taught the movement, whereas jogging does not have this learning curve.

The *Supercharger* can be performed in a variety of ways. We'll start with the easiest version. While marching in place, lifting knees about waist high, the opposing hand touches the raised knee (i.e., right hand touching raised left knee alternating with the left hand touching the raised right knee). This sounds simple enough, but you would be surprised by how many youngsters can't do this movement after being told what to do, seeing it done and even having their limbs physically manipulated by the instructor. Those youngsters who can't do such a simple movement are displaying a very weak connection between their brain hemispheres and will benefit greatly by learning and using/practicing this activity frequently. Learning the *Supercharger* has been shown to make all the difference in the world in terms of some children's readiness to learn. I've personally witnessed near miraculous transformations as the result of kids' learning/mastering this seemingly simple movement. Learning and practicing the *Supercharger* actually changes the structure and function of the brain of youngsters with a weak connection between the brain hemispheres.

Teaching the Supercharger:

To optimize benefits, before the academic component is added, the kids need to have mastered this movement so they can focus almost completely on the academics and not the movement itself. When doing **Brain Sprints**, stick with the basic 101 / jogging version until the youngsters have mastered the *Supercharger*. If the academics are added before the students are ready (i.e., have mastered the *Supercharger* movement), they will either mess up the academics or the cross-lateral movement.

Start by showing and explaining the *Supercharger and* its importance to the kids. Next, just watch for a few minutes to see who and how many are having trouble with it. If it is only a couple of youngsters having difficulty, maybe having a parent or teaching assistant take them into the hall to work with them individually is the better solution. If, however, there are several who can't grasp it and others who appear to be using all their brain power to hesitatingly get it, then here's the best solution we've found.

Put a sticker or small piece of masking tape on the back of one hand and another just above the knee on the opposing leg. Do this for all the students, as this works better than putting stickers on just a few students. Put stickers/ tape on yourself, too. Now show them how you are touching your hand with the sticker on it to the raised leg with a sticker on it and then the no-sticker hand to the sticker-less leg. Have them practice for a few minutes with you helping those who need assistance. The next day have them try the *Supercharger* without the stickers and assess where they are. Repeat the use of stickers if needed. This is well worth the time and effort involved because we are actually improving the structure and function of our youngsters' brains!

Combining the Academics with the *Supercharger*: Let's look at how to combine the *Supercharger* with basic math facts, such as 2 + 2 = 4. Simply touch the knees while saying the numbers and switch from one hand and knee to the others while saying, "plus" and "equals." If it's a single syllable answer as 4 is in this example, then say the answer twice (i.e., while one knee is being touched and then the other). For multi-syllable answers, as in 4 X 5 = 20, divide the answer into two parts; in this example that would be twen- and -ty. Touch one knee while saying "twen-"and the other knee while saying, "-ty." If this is confusing, simply check out the video at SmarterStrongerChildren.com or visit YouTube.com and type in "Brain Sprints Math" and watch the short Promo video.

For words/spelling simply touch a knee while saying each of the words and when saying the letters. For the word "house," as an example, it would go like this. You and the class say, "House – H-O-U-S-E spells house." In this case a knee is touched as you say each of the three words (i.e. *House*, *spells* and *house*) and as you say each of the five letters in the word "house." Continue in this fashion with three words and then do the sprinting as described in Brain Sprints 101 - SPELLING WORDS .

Tips:
There are several variations for the *Supercharger*. Here are some:

* While marching in place
* While skipping in place
* Elbows touching knees
* Seated – Elbows touching knees
* Forearms touching upper legs while marching or skipping

Keep the Brain Sprints fresh and super interesting by varying the *Supercharger* from seated one day to skipping the next to...

Modify to meet your needs or the needs of individual students. For example, a student who has just returned from being sick can stay seated and do a seated version of the *Supercharger,* touching hands or elbows to knees and then simulating the sprinting by pumping his/her arms quickly, as if actually sprinting.

These Brain Sprints are a great way to start reading or math class or to use whenever your youngsters need a break from seated activities. Use the charts at the end of this chapter or make up your own list of spelling words or equations. It really is as simple as displaying my list or your own, having the kids stand up beside their desks to start listening/stating and following along visually while *Supercharging* and then sprinting and REPEATING. The kids will love the Brain Sprints 2.0 and you for letting them do them!

Brain Sprints

3.0 / Jogging the Memory Version

Purpose:
Vocabulary/spelling or basic math facts, brain-power-boosting brain break, readiness to focus & learn

Grades:
First to fifth grade and up depending on the youngster(s) or group

Duration:
One to seven minutes – start with one or two minutes and increase time as ready for it – always keep them wanting more

Equipment Needed:
A numbered list of words or a lettered list of basic math facts displayed on a SMART board, dry-erase board, flip chart..., music and music player

How To:
In the previous versions of the Brain Sprints participants have alternated back and forth between two parts – the

jogging or *Supercharger* and the Sprinting. Brain Sprints 3.0 has three parts:

1. Practicing the math facts or the spelling of the words while doing the Supercharger.

2. Jogging the memory (the new part – explanation to come)

3. Sprinting

For the jogging-the-memory section:

For the math:

Use a strip of paper, a ruler...to cover the answers to the math equations. While the students are jogging in place, the instructor says a letter designating one of the three equations in this round of the Brain Sprints; the students then see how fast they can say the whole equation with the correct answer. Make a game of it by challenging them to see if they can be the first to give the answer / whole equation. After a reasonable length of time say, for example, "If you said 3 X 4 = 12, you are correct!" Repeat for a total of three equations and then proceed immediately to the sprinting. To avoid arguments as to who was first, do not recognize/point out a winner or winners AND quickly move on to the next equation or the sprinting. Another option is to challenge the students to see if they can be the first one to repeat each equation three times instead of the single time explained above.

For the Spelling:

Cover the words so the students can't see them. While the students are jogging in place, say one of the three words being used for this round of the Brain Sprints and have the youngsters spell it (each at his/her own pace). After a reasonable length of time say, for example, "If you spelled house, H-O-U-S-E, you are correct!" Repeat for a total of three words and then proceed immediately to the sprinting.

Make a game of it by challenging them to see if they can be the first to spell the word. To avoid arguments as to who was first, do not recognize/point out a winner or winners AND quickly move on to the next word or the sprinting.

Tips:

Here are two options. You can point out each word, letter or equation as you read them with the class, while a student stands in front of the room leading the *Supercharging*, jogging and sprinting; or you can actively participate with the students and as the leader of the *Supercharging*, jogging and sprinting while a selected student points out the words and letters or equations (to help direct their visual attention) as you and the class read/say them. To keep them more visually attentive, you can state the choices out of numerical/alphabetical order. Instead of pointing to the words and equations, you can simply call out the letter of the math fact to be practiced or the number of the word to be spelled.

By picking a different student each time based on merit and promising that everyone who does a good job will eventually get a chance to be the leader, the youngsters will have more of an incentive to do their very best.

In the place of spelling words, maybe create a list of words with their definitions and an example sentence of their use. Instead of spelling the word, they state the definition and/or use it in a sentence while *Supercharging;* state the definition from memory while jogging, and then say the designated word repeatedly while sprinting.

Optional: Put on some upbeat music to energize and better engage the class.

Modify to meet your needs or the needs of individual students. For example, a student who has just returned from being sick, can stay seated and do a seated version of the Supercharger and then pump his arms like he's jogging and sprinting.

These Brain Sprints *are* a great way to start reading or math class or to use whenever your youngsters need a break from seated activities. Use the charts at the end of this chapter or make up your own list of spelling words or equations. It really is as simple as displaying my list or your own, having the kids stand up beside their desks and start listening/ stating and following along visually while *Supercharging*, jogging, and then sprinting and REPEATING. The kids will love the Brain Sprints 3.0 and you for letting them do them!

Brain Sprints
Video Version

Purpose:
Basic math facts, brain-power-boosting brain break, readiness to focus & learn

Grades:
Primary grades and others depending on the youngster(s') or group's abilities and needs

Duration:
Two to seven minutes – start with about two minutes (one complete round of three equations – *Supercharger*, jogging and sprints) and increase time/rounds as ready for it – always keep them wanting more

Equipment Needed:

A computer or computer and Smart board at school and just a computer hooked up to the internet at home

How To:

On your computer go to YouTube.com or TeacherTube.com and type in "Brain Sprints Math." Select one of the four addition or subtraction basic facts videos and have your students follow the on-screen directions.

Tips:

There are three preparatory videos you may find valuable to watch before using the actual Brain Sprints math videos.

1. There is a 2-minute Promo video which is good for you and the kids to watch to see what the Brain Sprints are all about and to get them excited.

2. Another video for the adults explains why the Brain Sprints are an important addition to their children' development and education.

3. A third video is for the teacher and children to get them ready to get the most out of this powerful set of math videos.

Your enthusiasm and active participation will make these Brain Sprints video sessions very effective!

Modify to meet your needs or the needs of individual students. For example, a student who has just returned from being sick can stay seated and do a seated version of the Supercharger and then pump his arms like he's jogging and sprinting.

These Brain Sprints videos *are* a great way to start math class or to use whenever your youngsters need a break from seated activities. Use these videos often for best results and have fun with them.

When NOT using the videos, you can utilize the charts at the end of this chapter or make up your own list of spelling words or equations to use while doing the Brain Sprints 101, 2.0 and 3.0. It really is as simple as displaying my list or your own, having the kids stand up beside their desks and start listening/stating and following along visually while *Super-charging* their brain and muscles, jogging their memory and then sprinting to the answers and REPEATING. And it's even simpler with the 101 version where they only jog and sprint. Whichever version you use, the Brain Sprints videos or the other versions, the kids will love the Brain Sprints and you for letting them do them!

Brain Sprints Gets Results

Just the other day a teacher described her successful experience with a Brain Sprints video. She had forgotten to have her class exercise before the first half of a standardized test. At the end of the first half, the class enjoyed a Brain Sprints video break, followed immediately by the second half of the test. The bottom line: The class "scored 10% better after doing the Brain Sprints." It is common for students to be super focused and ready to learn AND do well on tests after brief Brain Sprints breaks.

Find Brain Sprints videos at:
YouTube.com, enter "Brain Sprints Math"
or "Ed Mayhew Brain Sprints" or visit
SmarterStrongerChildren.com

Brain Sprints

Addition Twos

A. $0 + 2 = 2$

B. $1 + 2 = 3$

C. $2 + 2 = 4$

D. $3 + 2 = 5$

E. $4 + 2 = 6$

F. $5 + 2 = 7$

G. $6 + 2 = 8$

H. $7 + 2 = 9$

I. $8 + 2 = 10$

J. $9 + 2 = 11$

K. $10 + 2 = 12$

L. $11 + 2 = 13$

Ed Mayhew

Brain Sprints

Multiplication Times Three

A. 1 x 3 = 3

B. 2 x 3 = 6

C. 3 x 3 = 9

D. 4 x 3 = 12

E. 5 x 3 = 15

F. 6 x 3 = 18

G. 7 x 3 = 21

H. 8 x 3 = 24

I. 9 x 3 = 27

J. 10 x 3 = 30

K. 11 x 3 = 33

L. 12 x 3 = 36

M. 0 x 3 = 0 (Bonus)

Brain Sprints

Vocabulary / Spelling

1. Den
2. Hen
3. Ken
4. Men
5. Pen
6. Ten
7. Open
8. Often
9. When
10. Kitten
11. Cop
12. Hop
13. Mop
14. Pop
15. Top
16. Shop
17. Clop
18. Gallop
19. Lollipop
20. Stop

CHAPTER THREE
Circle Up to Learn

Novelty is intricately associated with learning as the major "novelty center" of the brain (the SN/VTA) is linked closely with the learning and memory area (the hippocampus). **Brain Sprints** *give kids the novel learning experience AND advantage.*

In this chapter we'll look at two brain-power boosters that have the children standing in a circle around the room. The first has the students practicing and learning their basic math facts and the other one has them skip-counting by various numbers along with experiencing and understanding patterns. Both are potent and exciting brain-power boosters.

1. Circle Up to Learn
Basic Math Facts

Purpose:
Learn and practice basic math facts (addition, subtraction, multiplication & division), build cooperation and teamwork, give a brain-power-boosting brain break, enhance readiness to focus & learn

Grades:
First to fifth grade and up depending on the youngster(s) or group

Duration:
Two to seven minutes – start with two or three minutes and increase duration as ready for it – always keep them wanting more

Equipment Needed:
Optional – Two identical lettered lists of basic math facts or a set of counting-by-numbers (e.g., counting by twos – 2 to 36) displayed on a SMART board, dry-erase board, flip chart..., music and music player

How To:

1. Optional: Display two identical math facts charts on opposite sides of the room so that all the students can easily follow along with these visual ques. Although this step is optional, remember that vision is by far the most powerful of the five senses for learning.

2. Have the students form a circle around some of the

classroom furniture. There is usually no need to move the desks or other furniture.

3. Show them and have them practice this four-step sequence/pattern.

Step One:

The children touch their palms to the palms of the two students immediately to their left and right (a double high-five). They do this by raising both their hands, arms bent so that the fingers are pointing toward the ceiling, even with their ears and with the palms facing away from their faces. They then move their hands away from their own head just enough to tap the palms of their neighbors. When done right all the hands of all the kids are touching SIMULTANEOUSLY and for a brief instant.

Step Two:

Students clap their own hands a single time.

Step Three:

Repeat these two steps alternately and rhythmically.

Step Four:

When they can follow the two-step pattern rhythmically, add the math. Let's use 3 x 2 = 6 as our example.

A. Pat neighbors' hands while saying, "3"

B. Clap own hands while saying, "times"

C. Pat neighbors' hands while saying, "2"

D. Clap own hands while saying, "equals"

E. Pat neighbors' hands while saying, "6"

F. Clap own hands while repeating/saying, "6"

Now you are ready to repeat this pattern with the next equation (i.e. 3 x 3 = 9)

On single syllable answers such as 6, as in this example, we repeat the answer. On multi-syllable answers we divide the number/word. For 3 x 8 = 24, for example,

E. Pat (and hold an extra beat) neighbors' hands while saying, "Twenty-"

F. Clap own hands while saying, "-four"

That is, clap on the last syllable of multisyllable words/ numbers.

Tips:

For best results, you or another adult should actively participate as part of the circle.

For times three, for example, start with 3 x 0 = 0, or 3 x 1 = 3 and continue through this times table until you get to 3 x 12 = 36. Then quickly switch to the students sprinting in place while still in the circle formation. While they sprint, you state letters designating individual equations on the lettered list of equations. They repeatedly say the equation until you move their attention to another equation. Have them repeat each of the chosen equations two or three times or challenge them to see how fast they can say the equation three times – to see if they can be the first to say the equation three times. Have them sprint for no more than 20 to 30 seconds. Then return to the pat-clap pattern, starting with 3 x 12 = 36 and working back to 3 x 1 = 3, or 3 x 0 = 0. Follow up with more sprinting as described above.

Ed Mayhew

When performing the equations from memory (i.e. no math charts displayed), just say the equations you want them to repeat while sprinting.

Optional: Put on some music and encourage and lead them in rhythmically performing the pat-clap pattern to the rhythm of the music and then play some other more upbeat music during the sprinting to energize and optimize their sprinting.

Modify to meet your needs or the needs of individual students. For example, a student who has just returned from being sick can stay seated and still be included in the circle, and then pump his arms like he's sprinting during that part of the activity.

These *Circle Up to Learn* brain-power boosters are a great way to start math class or to use whenever your youngsters need a break from seated activities. Use the charts at the end of this chapter or make up your own list of equations. It really is as simple as displaying my list or your own, having the kids form a circle and performing the pat-clap pattern while saying the math equations and then sprinting and REPEATING. The kids will love this circle-up version of the Brain Sprints and you for letting them do them!

2. Circle Up to Learn
and Understand Skip Counting

Purpose:
Preparation for learning multiplication facts/tables, experiencing and understanding patterns, skip counting, cooperation and teamwork, brain-power-boosting brain break, enhancing readiness to focus & learn

Grades:
Kindergarten to fifth grade and up depending on the group's needs

Duration:
Two to seven minutes – start with two or three minutes and increase duration as ready for it – always keep them wanting more

Equipment Needed:
Optional – Two identical lists of counting by numbers (skip-counting numbers) displayed on a SMART board, dry-erase board, flip chart..., music and music player

How To:

1. OPTIONAL: post charts showing a list of numbers to be skip counted, on opposite sides of the room, so all students can easily follow along visually.

2. Have the students form a circle around some of the classroom furniture. There is usually no need to move the desks or other furniture.

3. Show them and have them practice the movement sequence/pattern. There are 11 different movement patterns (e.g. counting by 2s has its own unique movement pattern, as do 3s, 4s, etc.)

4. Add the counting (select from counting by 2s to counting by 12s and anything in between)

5. After they've finished counting a selected set of counting by numbers (e.g., 0, 2, 4, 6, 8, 10, 12, 14, 16, 18, 20), have them sprint in place (while staying in the circle formation) as you point to individual num-

bers on one of the charts for 20 to 30 seconds. Have them repeat the number you are pointing to over and over again until you choose a new number. Alternate between the counting-by-movement pattern with counting and the sprinting-in-place number repeating. If there are no charts, just tell them the numbers you want repeated during the sprinting. Optional: Have them alternate between counting forwards and counting backwards (i.e., 20, 18, 16, 14, 12, 10, 8, 6, 4, 2, 0 in this example).

6. Try any number of the 11 patterns / sets of counting-by-numbers to follow.

Circle Up to Count

by Twos/Twos Pattern

Step One:
Students clap their own hands a single time.

Step Two:
The children touch their palms to the palms of the two students immediately to their left and right (a double high-five). They do this by raising both their hands, arms bent so that the fingers are pointing toward the ceiling, even with their ears and with the palms facing away from their face. They then move their hands away from their own head just enough to tap the palms of their neighbors. When done correctly, all the hands of all the kids are touching SIMULTANEOUSLY and for a brief instant.

Step Three:
Repeat these two steps alternately and rhythmically.

Step Four:

When they can follow the two-step pattern rhythmically, add the counting like this.

    A. Clap own hands while WHISPERING, "One"

    B. Pat neighbors' hands while saying LOUDLY, "TWO!"

    C. Clap own hands while WHISPERING, "Three"

    D. Pat neighbors' hands while saying LOUDLY, "FOUR!"

    E. CONTINUE this way/pattern until get to 20 or your choice of an ending number

Tips:

For best results you or another adult should actively participate as part of the circle, leading them in rhythmically performing the Clap-Pat pattern.

Optional: Put on some upbeat music to energize the class during the interspersed optional sprinting in place.

Modify to meet your needs or the needs of individual students. For example, a student who has just returned from being sick can stay seated and still be included in the circle, clapping and patting and then pumping his arms like he's sprinting during that part of the activity.

Vocally EMPHASIZE the counting-by-twos numbers as pat neighbors' hands and deemphasize the in-between numbers by whispering these odd numbers. By including the whispered odd numbers in this way, they are learning what counting by twos (SKIP counting) really means. Of course, we can also switch from even to odd numbers EMPHASIZED / COUNTED as neighbors' hands are being patted (e.g. 1, 3, 5, 7 .)

These *Circle Up to Learn* brain-power boosters are a great way to start math class or to use whenever your youngsters need a break from seated activities. Use the charts at the end of this chapter or make up your own counting-by-numbers' list. It really is as simple as displaying my list or your own, having the kids form a circle and perform the Clap-Pat pattern while saying the numbers and then sprinting for 20 to 30 seconds between number sets and REPEATING. The kids will love this circle-up version of the Brain Sprints and you for letting them do them!

Circle Up to Count
by Threes / Threes Pattern

In this counting-by-threes pattern we add patting one's thighs to the clapping and patting neighbors' palms used in the previously discussed counting-by-twos pattern. Pat both thighs with your hands while bending the knees, as in a partial or slight squat. Straighten the legs for the clapping segment. These mini squats add a little more brain-power-boosting moderate exercise to the counting-by-threes pattern.

A. Pat thighs while WHISPERING, "One"

B. Clap own hands while WHISPERING, "Two"

C. Pat neighbors' hands while saying LOUDLY, "THREE!"

D. CONTINUE in this way/pattern until get to 36 or your choice of ending number

Tips:
For best results you or another adult should actively participate as part of the circle. When they've counted to 36 or

whatever ending number you've chosen, have them sprint in place for 20 to 30 seconds while saying the numbers at which you are pointing (or saying, if no chart). After the sprinting, they can repeat the counting / pattern for counting up from 3 to 36 or you can have them count backwards (i.e. 36 to 3). Then sprint again. Continue in this fashion for two to seven minutes. Modify to meet the needs of individual students or your group's readiness/needs.

Circle Up to Count

by Fours / Fours Pattern

For this counting-by-fours pattern we add a second pat of the thighs.

    A. Pat own thighs while WHISPERING, "One"

    B. Pat own thighs while WHISPERING, "Two"

    C. Clap own hands while WHISPERING, "Three"

    D. Pat neighbors' hands while saying LOUDLY, "FOUR!"

    E. CONTINUE in this way/pattern until get to 48 or your choice of ending number

Tips:

For best results you or another adult should actively participate as part of the circle. When they've counted to 48 or whatever ending number you've chosen, have them sprint in place for 20 to 30 seconds while saying the numbers at which you are pointing or which you are saying, if no chart. After the sprinting, they can repeat the counting / pattern for counting up from 4 to 48 or you can have them count backwards (i.e., 48 to 4). Then sprint again. Continue in this fashion for two to seven minutes. Modify to meet the needs of individual students or your group's readiness/needs.

Circle Up to Count
by Fives / Fives Pattern

When counting by fives we add a second clapping of the hands, making the pattern as follows:

A. Pat own thighs while WHISPERING, "One"

B. Pat own thighs while WHISPERING, "Two"

C. Clap own hands while WHISPERING, "Three"

D. Clap own hands while WHISPERING, "Four"

E. Pat neighbors' hands while saying EMPHATI-CALLY, "FIVE!"

F. CONTINUE in this way/pattern until get to 60 or your choice of ending number

Tips:

For best results you or another adult should actively participate as part of the circle. When they've counted to 60 or whatever ending number you've chosen, have them sprint in place for 20 to 30 seconds while saying the numbers at which you are pointing or which you are saying, if no chart. After the sprinting, they can repeat the counting / pattern for counting up from 5 to 60 or you can have them count backwards (i.e. 60 to 5). Then sprint again. Continue in this fashion for two to seven minutes. Modify to meet the needs of individual students or your group's readiness/needs.

Circle Up to Count
by Sixes / Sixes Pattern

For counting by sixes we add finger snapping in this fashion; cross the arms so that each wrist is in front of and close to its opposing shoulder, elbows bent, and immediately snap fingers on both hands. If can't snap fingers, then fake it.

A. Pat own thighs while WHISPERING, "One"

B. Pat own thighs while WHISPERING, "Two"

C. Clap own hands while WHISPERING, "Three"

D. Clap own hands while WHISPERING, "Four"

E. Cross wrists and snap fingers while WHISPERING, "Five"

F. Pat neighbors' hands while saying EMPHATI-CALLY, "SIX!"

G. CONTINUE in this way/pattern until get to 72 or your choice of ending number

Tips:

For best results you or another adult should actively participate as part of the circle. When they've counted to 72 or whatever ending number you've chosen, have them sprint in place for 20 to 30 seconds while saying the numbers at which you are pointing or which you are saying, if no chart. After the sprinting, they can repeat the counting / pattern for counting up from 6 to 72 or you can have them count backwards (i.e. 72 to 6). Then sprint again. Continue in this fashion for two to seven minutes. Modify to meet the needs of individual students or your group's readiness/needs.

Brand New Pattern

for Counting by Sevens to Twelves

For counting by sevens through twelves we have a whole new pattern of movements different from the pattern(s) for twos to sixes. The only two movements that remain are the finger snapping (used in every other pattern) and the patting of neighbors' hands (the double high-five). Here are the movements we'll be using:

- Supercharger – Marching in place and reaching across the body to touch one hand to the raised opposite knee and then touch the other knee with its opposing hand

- Hip Tap – Reaching across the body and touching one hand to the opposite hip and then reaching across the body to touch the other hip with the other hand

- Shoulder Tap – Reaching across the chest to touch one hand to the opposite shoulder and then using the other hand to tap the other shoulder

- Finger Snapping – Cross the arms so that each wrist is in front of and close to its opposing shoulder, elbows bent, and immediately snap fingers on both hands. If can't snap fingers, then fake it. ONLY USED FOR EVEN NUMBER COUNTING

- Heel Pat -- Touch the heel with opposite hand, BEHIND the knee of the leg one is standing on – heel's leg is bent at about a 90-degree angle (11s and 12s ONLY)

- Neighbor Pat – The children touch their palms to the palms of the two students immediately to their left and right (a double high-five). They do this by raising both their hands, arms bent so that the fingers are pointing toward the ceiling, even with their ears and with the palms facing away from their face. They then move their hands away from their own head just enough to tap the palms of their neighbors. When done correctly all the hands of all the kids are touching SIMULTANE-OUSLY and for a brief instant.

Circle Up to Count
by Sevens / Sevens Pattern

A. Touch one hand to raised opposite knee while WHISPERING, "One"

B. Touch other hand to raised opposite knee while WHISPERING, "Two"

C. Touch one hand to opposite hip while WHISPER-ING, "Three"

D. Touch other hand to opposite hip while WHISPER-ING, "Four"

E. Touch one hand to opposite shoulder while WHIS-PERING, "Five"

F. Touch other hand to opposing shoulder while WHISPERING, "Six"

G. Pat neighbors' hands while saying EMPHATI-CALLY, "SEVEN!"

H. CONTINUE in this way/pattern until get to 84 or your choice of ending number

Tips:

For best results you or another adult should actively participate as part of the circle. When they've counted to 84 or whatever ending number you've chosen, have them sprint in place for 20 to 30 seconds while saying the numbers at which you are pointing or which you are saying, if no chart. After the sprinting, they can repeat the counting / pattern for counting up from 7 to 84 or you can have them count backwards (i.e. 84 to 7). Then sprint again. Continue in this fashion for two to seven minutes. Modify to meet the needs of individual students or your group's readiness/needs.

Circle Up to Count
by Eights / Eights Pattern

A. Touch one hand to raised opposite knee while WHISPERING, "One"

B. Touch other hand to raised opposite knee while WHISPERING, "Two"

C. Touch one hand to opposite hip while WHISPERING, "Three"

D. Touch other hand to opposite hip while WHISPERING, "Four"

E. Touch one hand to opposite shoulder while WHISPERING, "Five"

F. Touch other hand to opposing shoulder while WHISPERING, "Six"

G. Cross wrists and snap fingers while WHISPERING, "Seven"

H. Pat neighbors' hands while saying EMPHATI-CALLY, "EIGHT!"

I. CONTINUE in this way/pattern until get to 96 or your choice of ending number

Tips:

For best results you or another adult should actively participate as part of the circle. When they've counted to 96 or whatever ending number you've chosen, have them sprint in place for 20 to 30 seconds while saying the numbers at which you are pointing or which you are saying, if no chart. After the sprinting, they can repeat the counting / pattern for counting up from 8 to 96 or you can have them count backwards (i.e., 96 to 8). Then sprint again. Continue in this fashion for two to seven minutes. Modify to meet the needs of individual students or your group's readiness/needs.

Circle Up to Count
by Nines / Nines Pattern

A. Touch one hand to raised opposite knee while WHISPERING, "One"

B. Touch other hand to raised opposite knee while WHISPERING, "Two"

C. Repeat A. touching hand to knee while WHISPER-ING, "Three"

D. Repeat B. touching hand to knee while WHISPER-ING, "Four"

E. Touch one hand to opposite hip while WHISPER-ING, "Five"

F. Touch other hand to opposite hip while WHISPER-ING, "Six"

G. Touch one hand to opposite shoulder while WHIS-PERING, "Seven"

H. Touch other hand to opposite shoulder while WHISPERING, "Eight"

I. Pat neighbors' hands while saying EMPHATI-CALLY, "NINE!"

J. CONTINUE in this way/pattern until get to 108 or your choice of ending number

Tips:

For best results you or another adult should actively partic-ipate as part of the circle. When they've counted to 108 or whatever ending number you've chosen, have them sprint in place for 20 to 30 seconds while saying the numbers at which you are pointing or which you are saying, if no chart. After the sprinting, they can repeat the counting / pattern for counting up from 9 to 108 or you can have them count backwards (i.e., 108 to 9). Then sprint again. Continue in this fashion for two to seven minutes. Modify to meet the needs of individual students or your group's readiness/needs.

Circle Up to Count
by Tens / Tens Pattern

A. Touch one hand to raised opposite knee while WHISPERING, "One"

B. Touch other hand to raised opposite knee while WHISPERING, "Two"

C. Repeat A. touching hand to knee while WHISPER-ING, "Three"

D. Repeat B. touching hand to knee while WHISPER-ING, "Four"

E. Touch one hand to opposite hip while WHISPER-ING, "Five"

F. Touch other hand to opposite hip while WHISPER-ING, "Six"

G. Touch one hand to opposite shoulder while WHIS-PERING, "Seven"

H. Touch other hand to opposite shoulder while WHISPERING, "Eight"

I. Cross wrists and snap fingers while WHISPERING, "Nine"

J. Pat neighbors' hands while saying EMPHATI-CALLY, "TEN!"

K. CONTINUE in this way/pattern until get to 120 or your choice of ending number

Tips:

For best results you or another adult should actively partic-ipate as part of the circle. When they've counted to 120 or whatever ending number you've chosen, have them sprint in place for 20 to 30 seconds while saying the numbers at which you are pointing or which you are saying, if no chart. After the sprinting, they can repeat the counting / pattern for counting up from 10 to 120 or you can have them count backwards (i.e., 120 to 10). Then sprint again. Continue in this fashion for two to seven minutes. Modify to meet the needs of individual students or your group's readiness/needs.

Circle Up to Count
by Elevens / Elevens Pattern

A. Touch one hand to heel of opposite foot* while WHISPERING, "One"

B. Touch other hand to heel of opposite foot* while WHISPERING, "Two"

C. Touch one hand to raised opposite knee while WHISPERING, "Three"

D. Touch other hand to raised opposite knee while WHISPERING, "Four"

E. Repeat C. touching hand to knee while WHISPERING, "Five"

F. Repeat D. touching hand to knee while WHISPERING, "Six"

G. Touch one hand to opposite hip while WHISPERING, "Seven"

H. Touch other hand to opposite hip while WHISPERING, "Eight"

I. Touch one hand to opposite shoulder while WHISPERING, "Nine"

J. Touch other hand to opposite shoulder while WHISPERING, "Ten"

K. Pat neighbors' hands while saying EMPHATICALLY, "ELEVEN!"

L. CONTINUE in this way/pattern until get to 132 or your choice of ending number

* Note: When touching the heel, it is BEHIND the knee of the leg one is standing on and the heel's leg is bent at about a 90-degree angle.

Tips:

For best results you or another adult should actively participate as part of the circle. When they've counted to 132 or whatever ending number you've chosen, have them sprint in place for 20 to 30 seconds while repeatedly saying the numbers at which you are pointing or which you are saying, if no chart. After the sprinting, they can repeat the counting / pattern for counting up from 11 to 132 or you can have them count backwards (i.e., 132 to 11). Then sprint again. Continue in this fashion for two to seven minutes. Modify to meet the needs of individual students or your group's readiness/needs.

Circle Up to Count
by Twelves / Twelves Pattern

A. Touch one hand to heel of opposite foot* while WHISPERING, "One"

B. Touch other hand to heel of opposite foot* while WHISPERING, "Two"

C. Touch one hand to raised opposite knee while WHISPERING, "Three"

D. Touch other hand to raised opposite knee while WHISPERING, "Four"

E. Repeat C. touching hand to knee while WHISPERING, "Five"

F. Repeat D. touching hand to knee while WHISPER-ING, "Six"

G. Touch one hand to opposite hip while WHISPER-ING, "Seven"

H. Touch other hand to opposite hip while WHISPER-ING, "Eight"

I. Touch one hand to opposite shoulder while WHIS-PERING, "Nine"

J. Touch other hand to opposite shoulder while WHISPERING, "Ten"

K. Cross wrists and snap fingers while WHISPERING, "Eleven"

L. Pat neighbors' hands while saying EMPHATI-CALLY, "Twelve!"

M. CONTINUE in this way/pattern until get to 144 or your choice of ending number

* Note: When touching the heel, it is BEHIND the knee of the leg one is standing on and heel's leg is bent at about a 90-degree angle.

Tips:

For best results, you or another adult should actively participate as part of the circle. When they've counted to 144 or whatever ending number you've chosen, have them sprint in place for 20 to 30 seconds while repeatedly saying the numbers at which you are pointing or which you are saying, if no chart. After the sprinting, they can repeat the counting / pattern for counting up from 12 to 144 or you can have them count backwards (i.e., 144 to

12). Then sprint again. Continue in this fashion for two to seven minutes. Modify to meet the needs of individual students or your group's readiness/needs.

Skip Counting

Partner Mirroring Style
(an option that doesn't require a class circle)

Purpose:
Skip counting / preparation for multiplication tables, cooperation and teamwork, brain-power-boosting brain break, readiness to focus & learning enhancement

Grades:
Kindergarten through fifth

Duration:
Two to seven minutes – start with two or three minutes and increase duration as ready for it – always keep them wanting more

Equipment Needed:
A list of counting-by-numbers displayed on a SMART board, dry-erase board, flip chart..., music and music player OPTIONAL

How To:

1. Display a list of numbers to be skip counted so all students can easily follow along visually.

2. Pair the students and have them face their partner and position them so that one of them can each see the

chart and can check to see that they count correctly (no class circle needed)

3. Show them and have them practice the movement sequence/pattern to be used for that particular counting-by-number. You'll find these movement patterns in the previous section of this chapter – Circle Up to Learn and Understand Skip Counting

4. Add the counting

5. After you've counted to a selected ending number for the skip-counting-by that you've chosen (e.g., counting by twos – 2, 4, 6, 8, 10, 12, 14, 16, 18, 20), have them face the chart and sprint in place as you point to individual numbers on the chart for 20 to 30 seconds. Have them repeat the number you are pointing to continually until you choose a new number at which to point.

6. REPEAT steps four and five for two to seven minutes, switching between counting forwards and backwards (e.g., 20, 18, 16, 14, 12, 10, 8, 6, 4, 2, for example) and the sprinting-number reciting.

7. Try any of the 11 patterns / sets of counting by numbers from 2's to 12' s. You'll find these 11 patterns described previously in this chapter. The only difference from the patterns described earlier and these is that instead of touching the hands to one's circle neighbors, the partners perform a two-hand pat with each other with hands level with the shoulders (and fingers pointing up, palms facing partner's, elbows bent) while EMPHATICALLY saying the equation's answer – See Circle Up to Learn and Understand Skip Counting earlier in this chapter for more detailed instructions).

**Find Brain Sprints videos at:
YouTube.com, enter "Brain Sprints Math"
or "Ed Mayhew Brain Sprints" or visit
SmarterStrongerChildren.com**

Circle Up to Learn

Sixes – Counting By & Multiplying Times

6	1 x 6 = 6
12	2 x 6 = 12
18	3 x 6 = 18
24	4 x 6 = 24
30	5 x 6 = 30
36	6 x 6 = 36
42	7 x 6 = 42
48	8 x 6 = 48
54	9 x 6 = 54
60	10 x 6 = 60
66	11 x 6 = 66
72	12 x 6 = 72

Circle Up to Learn

Sevens – Counting By & Multiplying Times

7	$1 \times 7 = 7$
14	$2 \times 7 = 14$
21	$3 \times 7 = 21$
28	$4 \times 7 = 28$
35	$5 \times 7 = 35$
42	$6 \times 7 = 42$
49	$7 \times 7 = 49$
56	$8 \times 7 = 56$
63	$9 \times 7 = 63$
70	$10 \times 7 = 70$
77	$11 \times 7 = 77$
84	$12 \times 7 = 84$

Circle Up to Learn

Twos – Counting By & Multiplying Times

2	1 X 2 = 2
4	2 X 2 = 4
6	3 X 2 = 6
8	4 X 2 = 8
10	5 X 2 = 10
12	6 X 2 = 12
14	7 X 2 = 14
16	8 X 2 = 16
18	9 X 2 = 18
20	10 X 2 = 20
22	11 X 2 = 22
24	12 X 2 = 24

Circle Up to Learn

Fives – Counting By & Multiplying Times

5	1 x 5 = 5
10	2 x 5 = 10
15	3 x 5 = 15
20	4 x 5 = 20
25	5 x 5 = 25
30	6 x 5 = 30
35	7 x 5 = 35
40	8 x 5 = 40
45	9 x 5 = 45
50	10 x 5 = 50
55	11 x 5 = 55
60	12 x 5 = 60

Circle Up to Learn

Tens – Counting By & Multiplying Times

10	1 X 10 = 10
20	2 X 10 = 20
30	3 X 10 = 30
40	4 X 10 = 40
50	5 X 10 = 50
60	6 X 10 = 60
70	7 X 10 = 70
80	8 X 10 = 80
90	9 X 10 = 90
100	10 X 10 = 100
110	11 X 10 = 110
120	12 X 10 = 120

CHAPTER FOUR
Partner Up to Learn

Frequent physical activity breaks, moderate to vigorous in intensity, improve students' readiness to focus, stay on task and learn. Both regular and single bouts of exercise have been shown to improve academic achievement.

The learning activities in this chapter require children to be put in pairs. Thus, besides their inherent brain-power-boosting qualities, they also promote cooperation and teamwork. They are so much fun and such an aid to learning that you and the kids will want to use them often.

Jump 'n Learn

Purpose:
Varied academics, basic math facts (addition, subtraction, multiplication & division), spelling, cooperation and team-

work, brain-power-boosting brain break, readiness to focus & learning enhancement, OPTIONAL – Race / timed challenge

Grades:
First to fifth grade and up depending on the youngster(s) or group & kindergarten (alphabetical & numerical sequencing)

Duration:
Two to six minutes – start with two or three minutes and increase duration as ready for it – always keep them wanting more

Equipment Needed:
Lettered list of non-sequential math equations, a numbered list of words/questions (or a list of sequenced letters & numbers in sets of three – for kindergarten only) displayed on a SMART board, dry-erase board, flip chart..., OPTIONAL: music and music player

How To:
1. Display a numbered list of questions with their answers, a lettered list of about 20 math equations, or a numbered list of about 20 words to be spelled – for kindergarteners, a numbered list of several sequenced pairs of letters / lettered list of sequenced pairs of numbers.

2. Pair each child with a partner. Let's call one child "A" and the other one "B".

3. For this example, "A" faces the displayed list of math equations and "B" has his/her back to the list. "A" reads the first equation without the answer and waits for "B's" answer. If "B" gives the correct answer, then "A" moves down the list to the next equation. When "B" gives a

wrong answer, "A" restates the equation with the correct answer and "B" must repeat/say the whole equation correctly before moving on to the next equation.

4. THE STUDENT BEING TESTED PRETENDS TO JUMP ROPE NONSTOP FOR THE DURATION OF HIS TURN. That is, continuously jumping/bouncing up and down on both feet while circling arms as if he were actually jumping rope.

5. Give the jumping partner 60 seconds, for example, to give answers to as many equations as he/she can and then switch roles so that the leader becomes the jumper / the tested (noncompetitive version).

6. OPTIONAL: Make it a competition where the emphasis is on each student's setting a new personal best. Say, "Go!" and time "B" for 30 seconds. At the end of 30 seconds, have "A" tell "B" his score (e.g., you got to equation F.). Then have "A" take a turn jumping nonstop and answering as many equations as can. Continue until each student has had two or more turns leading and two or more turns answering and thus two or three scores. Challenge each of them to see if with their second (and third?) turn they can beat their score from the first or second effort.

7. OPTIONAL: Have the pairs compete as a team of two. That is, combine their scores from their first run (e.g., "A" answered 5 equations and "B" 6 for a combined score of 11 on their first run) and try to beat that combined score during their second or third runs.

8. KINDERGARTEN: Since these youngsters may not be ready for math equations and spelling words, they can do alphabetical and numerical sequence problems/

challenges. In this case, "A" reads the first of two letters or numbers to the jumper. The jumping student answers with the next letter or number (e.g., F, G or 11, 12). In these examples, the one facing the chart says, "F, G" and the jumper is supposed to answer "H." For numbers example, the leader says, "11, 12" and the jumper says, "13." Leader corrects partner's mistakes or gives the answer if partner seems stuck.

Tips:
Put on some upbeat music if you think it would help. Adjust the duration of turns to best meet your students' abilities and needs (e.g., 45 second turns instead of 30-second ones). Emphasize the fun and benefit of attempting to set a new personal best, as opposed to always trying to beat another's score. If there is an uneven number of students, make one group of three or pair a student needing extra supervision with yourself.

OPTIONAL: Before putting students in pairs, have the whole class practice the *faux* rope jumping while you orally give them equations or questions to answer or words to spell.

Hand Jive Mathletics

Purpose:
Basic math facts (addition, subtraction, multiplication & division), experiencing and understanding patterns, cooperation and teamwork, brain-power-boosting brain break, readiness to focus & learning enhancement

Grades:
First to fifth grade and up depending on the youngster(s) or group

Duration:

Two to seven minutes – start with two or three minutes and increase duration as ready for it – always keep them wanting more

Equipment Needed:

A list of sequenced basic math facts (e.g., $0 + 2 = 2$; $1 + 2 = 3$; $2 + 2 = 4$...) displayed on a SMART board, dry-erase board, flip chart..., OPTIONAL: music and music player

How To:

Practice hand jive pattern without the math or the partners. In general terms, the pattern goes like this:

A. Extend RIGHT hand moving right to left in front of shoulders with fingers pointing up and palms facing away from self (arms stay bent at a 45 to 90-degree angle)

B. Clap own hands

C. Extend LEFT hand moving left to right in front of shoulders with fingers pointing up and palms facing away from self (arms stay bent at a 45 to 90-degree angle)

D. Clap own hands

E. Extend BOTH hands forward slightly (arms stay bent) in front of shoulders with fingers pointing up and palms facing away from self

F. Clap own hands

G. REPEAT this pattern until 'mastered'

Practice this movement sequence with the whole class moving in unison. Start very slowly – making sure all are performing the pattern correctly and pretending that are patting hands of a partner while practicing in unison. Then—

1. Put in groups of two and have practice this movement pattern until can do it well.

2. Display the list of sequenced math facts to be practiced.

3. Practice the pattern plus the math in pairs, but with the teacher leading whole class in unison and slowly at first, making sure all the partnerships have it. Use 6 + 4 = 10 as our sample. Touch right hands while saying, "6"; clap own hands while saying, "plus"; touch left hands while saying, "four"; clap own hands while saying, "equals"; touch both hands while saying, "ten"; AND clap own hands while repeating, "ten." If the ANSWER were a multi-syllable number, such as 11, then instead of repeating the answer (as done with single syllable numbers/sums, such as 10 in our example), the number/word is divided into two parts. In 11's case that's two-hand patting while saying, "elev-"and clapping own hands while saying, "-ven." When more than two syllables, hold two-handed pat an extra beat and clap on the last syllable (e.g., for 24, hold the two-handed pat while saying, "Twenty-" and clap on "-four" (the last or third syllable).

4. With one student in each twosome facing the chart (and checking to see that they are doing the math correctly) the pairs practice independent of the other twosomes.

5. Have students take turns facing the chart / checking the math.

Tips:

Emphasize building a nice rhythm. This may be better without the music so can move to own beat. Continue to check on the individual pairs to see that they are performing the hand jive correctly and continue helping those twosomes that need assistance until all are able to work independently.

OPTIONAL: Every couple of minutes have them stop the hand jiving and do a 20- to 30-second all-out sprinting in place while saying the equations you point to on the chart.

Hand Jive Math

for PRIMARY STUDENTS

Purpose:

Basic math facts (addition, subtraction), experiencing and understanding patterns, cooperation and teamwork, brain-power-boosting brain break, enhancing readiness to focus & learn

Grades:

First and second (some kindergarteners later in the year)

Duration:

Two to six minutes – start with two or three minutes and increase duration as ready for it – always keep them wanting more

Equipment Needed:

A list of sequenced basic math facts (e.g. $0 + 2 = 2$; $1 + 2 = 3$; $2 + 2 = 4$...) displayed on a SMART board, dry-erase board, flip chart..., OPTIONAL: music and music player

How To:

1. Practice hand jive pattern without the math or partners. In general terms, the pattern goes like this:

   A. Extend BOTH hands forward slightly (arms stay bent) in front of shoulders with fingers pointing up and palms facing away from self

   B. Clap own hands

   C. REPEAT this "A" "B" Pattern
      Practice this movement with the whole class moving in unison. Start very slowly – making sure all are performing the pattern correctly. In step "A" they pretend that they are patting hands of a partner while practicing.

   D. Put in groups of two and have practice this movement pattern until can do it well. In step "A" partners touch each other's hands/palms.

2. Practice with the math. It goes like this for 4 + 2 = 6:

   A. Touch partner's hands with both hands while saying, "4"

   B. Clap own hands while saying, "plus"

   C. Touch partner's hands with both hands while saying, "2"

   D. Clap own hands while saying, "equals"

   E. Touch partner's hands with both hands while saying, "6"
      Clap own hands while saying/repeating, "6". If the answer is a multi-syllable number, such as 24, then instead of repeating the answer (as done with single syllable numbers/sums, such as 6 in our example),

the number/word is divided into two parts. In 24's case that's two-hand patting (and holding an extra beat) while saying, "twenty-"and clapping own hands on the LAST syllable while saying, "-four".

F. Practice the pattern plus the math while in pairs, but with the teacher leading whole class in unison and slowly at first, making sure all the partnerships have it.

G. With one student in each twosome facing the chart (and checking to see that are doing the math correctly) the pairs practice independent of the other twosomes.

H. Have students/partners take turns facing the chart / checking the math.

Tips:

Start by demonstrating the *Hand Jive* (including the math component) with a partner.

Emphasize building a nice rhythm. This may be better without the music so can move to own beat. Continue to check on the individual pairs to see that they are performing the hand jive correctly and continue helping those twosomes that need assistance until all are able to work independently.

OPTIONAL: Every couple of minutes have them stop the hand jiving and do a 20- to 30-second all-out sprint in place while saying the equations you point to on the chart.

Hand-to-Hand Combat

Purpose:

Preview or review what facts students know, fun competition, brain-power-boosting brain break, enhancing readiness to focus & learn

Grades:

Fourth grade and up depending on the group's readiness

Duration:

Two to six minutes – start with two or three minutes and increase duration as ready for it – always keep them wanting more

Equipment Needed:

A ready series of true/false statements, optional – a slide show / power point presentation that allows for displaying one true/false statement at a time on a SMART board, OPTIONAL: music and music player

How To:

1. Put students into pairs.

2. One child in each twosome is "TRUE" and the other one is 'FALSE."

3. Have the two students to stand and face each other. Their arms are bent (with elbows near own sides) and extended in front of them. Palms are facing down and fingers are within an inch of opponent's fingers, but not touching.

4. Explain that you are going to say a statement that is true or false. You will repeat the statement and give them time to decide if they think the statement is true or false. Tell them that on the signal, "GO" they will either "attack" or "retreat." That is, if the statement is true, TRUE will try to slap FALSE'S hands before he can pull them back to his body. If the statement is false, however, then FALSE will try to slap TRUE'S hands

before he can pull them back out of the way. A point is scored for successfully hitting the hands of the opponent before he can "escape" or for successfully avoiding getting slapped/tagged. No point is awarded if the wrong person attacks / the wrong person escapes.

5. Tell the opponents to stay perfectly still so as not to give away whether they are getting ready to attack or escape. Also, no steps are allowed (i.e., all movement is done with the arms and hands alone).

Toss 'n Count

Purpose:
Skip count, basic math facts (addition, subtraction, multiplication, division), eye-hand coordination, cooperation and teamwork, brain-power-boosting brain break, enhancing readiness to focus & learn

Grades:
First through fifth (kindergarteners – 1's, 5's & 10's)

Duration:
Two to six minutes – start with two or three minutes and increase duration as ready for it – always keep them wanting more

Equipment Needed:
A list of counting by numbers or sequenced basic math facts displayed on a SMART board, dry-erase board, flip chart..., a ball for each twosome, OPTIONAL: music and music player

How To:

1. Display a sequenced list of counting by numbers (e.g., 5, 10, 15, 20...) or sequenced math facts (e.g., 0 +2 = 2; 1 + 2 = 3; 2 + 2 = 4...).

2. Put students in pairs and give each twosome a ball.

3. Have them practice throwing the ball underhanded to each other and so that the partner can catch the ball most of the time.

4. Add the math: Using the chart as needed, have them say the next number before throwing the ball (e.g., when counting by 2's if their partner just said, "8," then they would say, "10." For math equations, they say the next number or word before throwing (e.g., For 7 x 8 = 56, if their partner just said, "8," then they would say, "equals." That is, before each toss they say the next number or symbol/word in the equation. Or they can have to say the next whole equation on the list before tossing the ball.

5. Encourage them to develop a quick rhythmical game of toss while saying the math.

Tips:

The best balls for this are ones that are not very bouncy and don't roll easily when they hit the floor. The PE department may have yarn balls that have these qualities that you can borrow. The local dollar store may have inexpensive balls that meet this criterion. Or invite the students to bring in their stuffed animals that they don't mind having tossed around; you only need half the class to bring one in.

Another inexpensive option is to ball up sheets of newspaper and wrap in tape to keep their spherical shape.

Optional: Every couple of minutes stop the toss 'n counting and play some lively music to energize them while they perform 20 to 30 seconds of sprinting in place, all the while reciting the counting by numbers or the math equations.

Toss 'n Spell

Purpose:
Spelling / vocabulary words, eye-hand coordination, cooperation and teamwork, brain-power-boosting brain break, enhancing readiness to focus & learn

Grades:
First through fifth (kindergarteners – later in the schoolyear?)

Duration:
Two to six minutes – start with two or three minutes and increase duration as ready for it – always keep them wanting more

Equipment Needed:
A list of words displayed on a SMART board, dry-erase board, flip chart ..., a ball for each twosome, OPTIONAL: music and music player

How To:
1. Display a list of words to be spelled

2. Put students in pairs and give each twosome a ball.

3. Have them practice throwing the balls underhanded and so that their partner can catch the ball most of the time.

4. Add the spelling: Using the chart as needed, have them say the next letter before throwing the ball (e.g. when spelling "cat," if their partner just said, "a," then they would say, "t." After "t" they say the word just spelled, in this case "cat." But they don't say it just once, but they say it in unison 5 times; one time with each of five quick jumps (i.e., they say, "Cat, cat, cat, cat, cat" as they jump up quickly five times). Immediately after the fifth jump / fifth reciting of the word spelled, they start tossing /spelling the next word on the list.

5. Encourage them to develop a quick rhythmical game of toss while spelling the words.

Optional: Instead of a list of words, give them a sentence or phrase whose words they spell (e.g., spell the words in this sentence: Mrs. Roberts' class rocks and spells with the best!) Make this a competition to see which twosome can finish first, second and third, for example.

Tips:

The best balls for this are ones that are not very bouncy and don't roll easily when they hit the floor. The PE department may have yarn balls that have these qualities that you can borrow. The local dollar store may have inexpensive balls that meet this criterion. Or invite the students to bring in any stuffed animals that they don't mind having tossed around; you only need half the class to bring one in.

Another option is to ball up sheets of newspaper and wrap in tape to keep their spherical shape.

Optional: Play some lively music that will energize the class.

Modify to meet your needs or the needs of individual students. For example, a student who has just returned from being sick, can stay seated and still be included by moving his arms up and down during the jumping portion of the *Toss 'n Spell.*

Back-to-Back Math

Purpose:
Math (addition, subtraction, multiplication), cooperation and teamwork, brain-power-boosting brain break, enhancing readiness to focus & learn

Grades:
First through fifth

Duration:
Two to seven minutes – start with two or three minutes and increase duration as ready for it – always keep them wanting more

Equipment Needed:
None - OPTIONAL: music and music player

How To:
1. Put students in pairs according to their math ability

2. Have the partners stand back to back. Then have them practice bouncing (small jumps) three times and then jump-turning to face partner (i.e. bounce, bounce, bounce, jump-turn).

3. Adding the math: Prior to the bouncing, have them hold one hand close to and in front on their chest and choose to hold up one to five fingers on that hand.

When they have jump-turned to face each other the first one to say the total number of fingers held up (addition) wins that round. For example, one partner is holding up 2 fingers and the other one is holding up 3 – the answer is "5!"

4. When they've mastered the game using only one hand each, have them try holding up fingers on both hands. After addition, move on to subtraction and multiplication.

Tips:

In the beginning, lead them by telling them to choose how many fingers to hold up and then saying, "Ready, bounce, bounce, bounce, jump-turn!" When they have the pattern down, let the pairs work independently. Have them change partners every minute or two.

If there is an odd number of students, you can partner up with the student who needs the most help. Another option is to have one group of three students, which means they would be adding three numbers instead of two (e.g., $3 + 4 + 2 = 9$). For that matter, this can be a threesome game instead of a partner game which would put *Back-to-Back Math* in with the small group activities (chapter 5).

Optional: Play some lively music to energize the class and have them do 20 to 30 seconds of sprinting in place (while reciting math equations) every couple of minutes to add more aerobic benefits.

Find Brain Sprints videos at:
YouTube.com, enter "Brain Sprints Math"
or "Ed Mayhew Brain Sprints" or visit
SmarterStrongerChildren.com

CHAPTER FIVE

Small Groups to Learn

Scientists at Johns Hopkins put accelerometers on approximately 12,500 individuals and had them wear them for seven days. They found that more than a third of 6 to 11-year-olds and almost two-thirds of those aged 12 to 19 were NOT getting the CDC's and the WHO's highly recommended 60 minutes of daily brain-power-boosting, overall well-being producing moderate-to-vigorous physical activity – 2017 study report

A major advantage of having several small groups over having one large group (think, whole class) is that each youngster gets more turns. Less waiting for a turn means less boredom, less off-task behavior and more learning taking place. The disadvantage is that it can be harder to manage so many groups at once. However, as you will see when you try these smaller groupings, you'll enjoy a more energetic and engaged bunch of students.

Triple Toss Learning

Purpose:
Varied academics (learning, practicing or reviewing), eye-hand coordination, cooperation and teamwork, brain-power-boosting brain break, enhancing readiness to focus & learn

Grades:
First through fifth (kindergarteners – maybe later in the schoolyear)

Duration:
Three to six minutes – start with about three minutes and increase duration as ready for it – always keep them wanting more

Equipment Needed:
A numbered or lettered list of questions / math problems or equations with their answers displayed on a SMART board, dry-erase board, flip chart…, a ball for each threesome, OPTIONAL: music and music player

How To:
1. Display a list of questions / math problems or equations with their answers

2. Put students in threesomes and give each group a ball. Arrange each group so that one is facing the display and the other two are side-by-side a few feet from each other with their backs to the questions and answers

3. Have them practice throwing the balls underhanded and so that their partners can catch the ball most of the time.

4. COOPERATION MODEL: This can be a competitive or a cooperative activity. Let's start with working as a team. The leader (facing the chart) reads the first question. The other two then talk it over and come up with an agreed-upon answer. If the answer is correct, they get to toss the ball around the triangle so that each gets to throw and catch a single time. If their answer is wrong, the leader tells them the answer and then moves on to the next question without their getting to toss and catch the ball. The leader gets to do three questions and then they rotate so that there is a new leader for the next three problems. They keep rotating in this fashion for the length of the activity.

5. COMPETITION MODEL: Same as 4, except that the two with their backs to the questions are competing with each other to see who can come up with the correct answer first. In this version, the leader plays catch (throws and catches a single time) with the one who correctly answered first. Then he moves on to the next question. If neither answers correctly, then there is no tossing of the ball and the leader tells the other two the answer and moves on to the next question. If the leader can't determine who answered first, he calls it a tie and throws the ball to each player. The teacher controls the rotation of players by giving each leader one minute before having them rotate for a new leader.

Tips:
The best balls for this are ones that are not very bouncy and don't roll easily when they hit the floor. The PE department may have yarn-like balls that have these qualities that you can borrow. The local dollar store may have inexpensive balls that meet this criterion. Or invite the

students to bring in any stuffed animals that they don't mind having tossed around; you only need one-third of the class to bring one in.

Another option is to ball up sheets of newspaper and wrap in tape to keep their spherical shape.

Optional: Play some lively music to energize the class as they interject/do 20- to 30-seconds of sprinting in place every couple of minutes. While they are sprinting ask them a couple of the questions and have them answer in unison.

Triangular Toss 'n Word Play

Purpose:
Vocabulary words/definitions/spelling, eye-hand coordination, cooperation and teamwork, brain-power-boosting brain break, enhancing readiness to focus & learn

Grades:
First through fifth

Duration:
Two to six minutes – start with two or three minutes and increase duration as ready for it – always keep them wanting more

Equipment Needed:
A numbered list of a few definitions and a list of matching vocabulary words (in random order) displayed on a SMART board, dry-erase board, flip chart..., a ball for each threesome, OPTIONAL: music and music player

How To:

1. Display a numbered list of three definitions followed by the three matching words in random order

2. Put students in threesomes and give each group a ball. Arrange each group so that they are a few feet apart from each other for tossing purposes.

3. Have them practice throwing the balls underhanded and so that their partners can catch the ball most of the time.

4. COOPERATION MODEL: This can be a competitive or a cooperative activity. Let's start with the noncompetitive approach. The group of three decides which of the three words is defined in definition 1. and proceeds to spell the word while tossing the ball around the circle. More precisely, before each player throws the ball he/she says the next letter of the word being spelled. When they have spelled the word, they all jump up, clap their hands over head and say the word five times in unison (i.e., they say the word once with each of the five jumps/claps). Then they do the same thing for definitions 2 and 3. When most or all of the groups are done, review / go over the correct matches and then put up another set of three definitions and their matching words to try. Note: During the jumps/claps, the student with the ball can do modified claps with the ball in her hand.

5. COMPETITION MODEL: Same as 4, except that each trio of students is competing with the other threesomes to match and spell the three words the fastest. They start when the teacher says, "GO!" The first group to finish spelling the third word and saying it five times

with the jumps/claps, immediately says, "DONE!" The teacher then quizzes them as to whether they matched the words to their definitions correctly. If they did, they are declared the winners.

Tips:

The best balls for this are ones that are not very bouncy and don't roll easily when they hit the floor. The PE department may have yarn-like balls that have these qualities that you can borrow. The local dollar store may have inexpensive balls that meet this criterion. Or invite the students to bring in any stuffed animals that they don't mind having tossed around; you only need one-third of the class to bring one in.

Another inexpensive option is to ball up sheets of newspaper and wrap in tape to keep their spherical shape.

Optional: Play some lively music to energize the class as they do 20- to 30-seconds of sprinting in place after completing each round of three definitions/words. While they are sprinting say one of the three words or definitions and have them answer in unison the matching word or definition.

Valentine's Day Toss

Purpose:

Language arts, fun Valentine's-Day-themed activity, eye-hand coordination, cooperation and teamwork, brain-power-boosting-brain break, enhancing readiness to focus & learn

Grades:

First through fifth

Duration:

Two to six minutes – start with two or three minutes and increase duration as ready for it – always keep them wanting more

Equipment Needed:

A ball for each group of 4 or 5 students, OPTIONAL: music and music player

How To:

1. Put students in groups of 4 or 5 students each and give each group a ball. Arrange each group so that there is one leader (with the ball) facing the other 3 or 4 players who are in a line side by side a few feet away from the leader for tossing purposes.

2. Have groups practice throwing the balls underhanded and so that the members of their group can catch the ball most of the time.

3. Teacher names a topic, such as food, game or person and instructs the students that they are to say a complete SENTENCE that contains the word "like" or "love."

4. The leader acknowledges the first player in line. That person then says what they like or love. If the student says a complete sentence with the word like or love in it, then the leader plays catch with that student (i.e., one toss and catch each). For example, if the topic is food, the student says, "I love macaroni and cheese!" Then the leader plays catch with that player. If, however, the student just says, "Macaroni and cheese!" – then the leader does not toss him the ball. The leader goes down the line of players in this fashion until

everyone in the line has had a turn. Then the leader joins the line and the last person in line rotates to be the new leader.

5. When each student has had a turn or two with the first topic, the teacher picks a new topic. Topics can range from superhero /cartoon character, to a place, to what like/love best about school, etc. When the class gets the hang of this, the leader in each group can choose the new topic.

Tips:

The best balls for this are ones that are not very bouncy and don't roll easily when they hit the floor. The PE department may have yarn-like balls that have these qualities that you can borrow. The local dollar store may have inexpensive balls that meet this criterion. Or invite the students to bring in any stuffed animals that they don't mind having tossed around; you only need one-third of the class to bring one in.

Another inexpensive option is to ball up sheets of news-paper and wrap in tape to keep their spherical shape.

Optional: Play some lively music to energize the class as they do 20 to 30 seconds of sprinting in place after completing each teacher-chosen topic. While they are sprinting have them say sentences related to the topic (e.g., If the topic is food, they might say: "I love spinach! I love chocolate ice cream! I really like popcorn! I love _____..."

Toss, Jump 'n Shout

Purpose:

Skip counting/preparation for multiplication tables / spelling, eye-hand coordination, cooperation and teamwork, brain-power-boosting brain break, enhancing readiness to focus & learn

Grades:
First through fifth

Duration:
Two to six minutes – start with two or three minutes and increase duration as ready for it – always keep them wanting more

Equipment Needed:
A list of counting-by numbers or list of words displayed on a SMART board, dry-erase board, flip chart..., a ball for each group (2 to 6 balls), OPTIONAL: music and music player

How To:
1. Display either a list of counting by numbers or words to spell depending on whether you choose to have them do counting or spelling

2. Put students in small circles of four to six students (or divide the class into two groups/circles) and give each group a ball. Arrange each circle so that students are a few feet apart from each other for tossing purposes.

3. Have them practice throwing the balls underhanded, from person to person, around the circle and so that their circle mates can catch the ball most of the time.

4. COOPERATION MODEL: This can be a competitive or a cooperative activity. Let's start with the cooperative one. Designate one person in each circle to be the leader. The leader starts with the ball and starts

it going around the circle with each member passing the ball to the person beside him/her until it gets back to the leader. Depending on whether they are spelling words or counting, each time the ball gets back to the leader, the whole group jumps and claps hands overhead one or more times while saying the appropriate letters or numbers with each jump/clap. Note: The leader claps as best she can while holding the ball. FOR SPELLING: Let's use the word "Liberty" as an example. The first time the ball gets back to the leader, the whole circle jumps up/claps and says in unison "L," the second time the ball gets back to the leader they jump up / clap twice while saying in unison "L-i," (that is, one letter with each jump). They continue adding one more jump with each new letter until they have spelled the whole word, ("liberty" in this case). When they get to the last letter, "y," they will be jumping up seven times because there are seven letters in "liberty." Then the ball is passed around one last time and the word is spelled again and the word itself is stated with an eighth jump (a grand total of 36 jump/claps). Then they move on to the next word to be spelled and follow the same pattern. FOR SKIP COUNTING: For counting by numbers, let's use counting by sevens as our example. The first time the ball gets back to the leader, they all jump/clap a single time while saying in unison, "7," and the next time the ball has gone around the circle, they jump/clap two times while saying, "7, 14." They continue in this fashion until they get to 84 or whatever the chosen ending number is (i.e., when they get to 84, they jump up/clap/say the 12 counting-by-sevens numbers twelve times for a grand total of 78 jumps – a good and fun workout). Just to be clear, at 7 they jump up once; at 7, 14 they make two jumps; at 7, 14, 21 they jump three times and they are always saying a single number with each jump/clap.

5. COMPETITION MODEL: Same as 4, except that each circle of students is competing with the other groups to spell a given word or list of words or complete a set of counting by numbers the fastest. They start when the teacher says, "GO!" The first group to finish spelling the word or group of words or finish counting (e.g. from 3 to 36 by 3s, immediately says, "DONE!" They are the winning group. This competitive version works best when the class is divided into just two circles. Having an adult leading each circle is also helpful.

Tips:

The best balls for this are ones that are not very bouncy and don't roll easily when they hit the floor. The PE department may have yarn-like balls that have these qualities that you can borrow. The local dollar store may have inexpensive balls that meet this criterion. Or invite the students to bring in any stuffed animals that they don't mind having tossed around – you only need a few members of the class to bring one in.

Another inexpensive option is to ball up sheets of newspaper and wrap in tape to keep their spherical shape.

To add variety, interest and improve dexterity have them pass the ball around their back or under one leg and then the other before passing it to the next person. If the class has trouble with tossing and catching the balls, switch to handing the ball to one's neighbor.

Optional: Play some lively music while they do 20 to 30 seconds of sprinting in place between words or each set of counting by numbers (e.g., counting from 3 to 36, by threes).

While they are sprinting, point to one of the numbers and have them repeat it until you point to another number, or have them spell the word you are pointing to and/or naming.

Wits-About-You Ball Race

Purpose:
General academics, quick thinking under pressure, eye-hand coordination, cooperation and teamwork, brain-power-boosting brain break, enhancing readiness to focus & learn

Grades:
Kindergarten through fifth

Duration:
Two to eight minutes – start with two or three minutes and increase duration as ready for it – always keep them wanting more

Equipment Needed:
Two balls for each group (4 to 8 balls), OPTIONAL: music and music player

How To:
1. Put students in small circles of about six students and give each group 2 balls. Arrange each circle so that the students are a few feet apart from each other for tossing purposes.

2. Have them practice handing the balls to their circle neighbors as they pass the balls around the circle.

3. Start with the two balls on opposite sides of the circle of about 6 youngsters. The balls are passed in the same direction around the circle (i.e., either clockwise or counterclockwise). Before a student can pass/handoff the ball, he/she must come up with and say an appropriate answer. For example, they must name an animal, but they can't name the same animal on consecutive turns and they are not allowed to say the same animal as the person just before them. Other possible topics are foods in general, vegetables, forms of transportation, states...If one of the balls catches up with the other, whoever is caught with both balls must exit the circle. They get back in as soon as someone else goes out or after they've gone back to their desk and written three correct answers (for younger children they've told the teacher three answers). If this is not working well (i.e., the balls are catching up to one another too often because the kids can't think fast enough under pressure) you may need larger circles. For kindergarteners, a single whole class circle starting with two balls and adding a third and then a fourth ball as ready works best.

Tips:

The best balls for this are ones that are not very bouncy and don't roll easily when they hit the floor. The PE department may have yarn-like balls that have these qualities that you can borrow. The local dollar store may have inexpensive balls that meet this criterion. Or invite the students to bring in any stuffed animals that they don't mind having tossed around; you only need one-third or so of the class to bring one in.

Another option is to ball up sheets of newspaper and wrap in tape to keep their spherical shape.

Optional: Play some lively music and have them do 20 to 30-seconds of sprinting in place every couple of minutes.

While they are sprinting have them see how many answers they can state for the topic being used or about to be used (e.g., topic vegetables – they say things like beets, carrots, spinach, cucumber...).

Criss-Cross Ball Toss

Purpose:
Counting by twos (odd & even numbers), eye-hand coordination, cooperation and teamwork, brain-power-boosting brain break, enhancing readiness to focus & learn

Grades:
Kindergarten through fifth

Duration:
Two to six minutes – start with two or three minutes and increase duration as ready for it – always keep them wanting more

Equipment Needed:
Two balls for each group (4 to 8 balls), OPTIONAL: music and music player

How To:
1. Put students in small circles of about eight students and give each group 2 balls.

2. Have them practice passing the two balls around the circle in opposite directions by handing the ball to their immediate circle neighbor on their right or left.

3. Start with the two balls on opposite sides of the circle

of about 8 youngsters. The balls are passed in opposite directions around the circle so that the balls cross (i.e., pass each other going in opposite directions) two times per lap. Each time the balls crisscross/pass each other, the whole group says in unison the count. For example, the first time the two balls cross, the kids say, "2;" the next crisscrossing they say, "4'" They continue to 20 or whatever ending number you have chosen. The first team to get to 20 or ____ wins the race.

Tips:

The best balls for this are ones that are not very bouncy and don't roll easily when they hit the floor. The PE department may have yarn-like balls that have these qualities that you can borrow. The local dollar store may have inexpensive balls that meet this criterion. Or invite the students to bring in any stuffed animals that they don't mind having tossed around; you only need about one-fourth of the class to bring one in.

Another option is to ball up sheets of newspaper and wrap in tape to keep their spherical shape.

Instead of counting even numbers they can count odd numbers (i.e. 1, 3, 5, 7...to 25 or ____). Of course, they could count by 3's, 4's, etc.

For kindergarteners, it is best to have just one whole-class noncompetitive circle. You can have two or more circles competing if there is an adult to lead each one.

Optional: Play some lively music while they do 20 to 30 seconds of sprinting in place right after each race. While they are sprinting ask them, when counting by twos, what number comes right after 4 or what's the next number after 14 or what number is right before 12, etc.

The Line Up

Purpose:
General academics, money, place value, spelling, quick thinking under pressure, cooperation and teamwork, brain-power-boosting brain break, enhancing readiness to focus & learn

Grades:
Kindergarten through fifth

Duration:
Two to ten minutes – start with two or three minutes and increase duration as ready for it – always keep them wanting more

Equipment Needed:
Two or more sets of large number or letter cards, OPTIONAL: music and music player

How To:

1. Make two identical sets of cards about 5"x5" out of card stock or paper with one numeral or letter on each card (For numbers: Make cards for all 10 numerals - 0 to 9 - and decimal points and dollar and cents signs if needed; for spelling words: only make cards with the letters they'll need for the words they are to spell).

2. Divide the class into three groups of equal size and abilities. Each team needs a leader whose job it is to see that their team picks up the right cards and gets in the correct order.

3. In this game two teams race to find the needed number or letter cards to form the correct word or number answer. Once they have found the needed letters or numbers (that were face down in front of them on the floor or on a table), they stand side by side with each one holding a card in front of his/her chest so that the letters or numbers are right side up and in the right order to spell the word or form the correct number (sometimes one student will need to hold two cards or two students will hold one card). The leader does not hold a card, but checks to see that the cards are right side up and in the right order. For our SPELLING example let's have the teacher say, "The organ with which you think. GO!" The first team to hold the cards correctly to spell "BRAIN" would win. The third team judges to see who finishes first and if the word or number is correct. The team that wins stays and the judges and losing team trade places so that the winning team has a new team to challenge them. This fun game is great for practicing/learning place value, money, general academics and spelling.

4. PLACE VALUE: You need two sets of 10 cards each (i.e. two sets of 0 to 9) with optional comma cards. Spread the cards out on the floor in front of the two teams (one set in front of each team) cards facing down so that the numbers are not visible. Let's say the teacher says, for example, "1, 493." Then on "Go!" the students pick up the cards and get in order of 1,493. Whichever team finishes first with the CORRECT number, wins. All teammates need to be holding a card – so sometimes two students will be holding one card between them. Since younger children

may only be ready for the ones and tens place, they may be put into 6 teams of three students each, for example; in this case three teams of three compete while the other three judge. One of the three teammates is the leader and doesn't hold a card. In this case you'll need three sets of cards. Kindergarteners would do number order and stand one behind the other holding the cards in 1, 2, 3...order or alphabetical order (e.g., D, E, F, G).

5. MONEY: You need two sets of cards 0 to 9 plus a decimal point and dollar sign (and maybe a cent sign). Same as place value except the teacher says, "one dollar -ninety-seven cents" and the kids hold the cards to form $1.97.

6. GENERAL ACADEMICS: You'll need two sets of letter cards. The teacher says, for example, "a four-letter word for a part of your head or face. GO!" the kids then can spell "nose" or "chin or "ears,' or ____. You can use this for social studies, science, math words, etc.

Tips:

For some word or number answers you'll need to have duplicate numbers or letters in each set of cards (e.g., two 3's, two D's...in each set for answers such as, 3,347 or PADDLE).

Optional: Play some lively music while the class does 20 to 30 seconds of sprinting in place after each race. While they are sprinting have them answer questions from the previous game. For example, if the answer was 204, ask them what is the last number in 204; what's the silent number in 204; which numeral is in the tens place, etc.

Do You See What I See?

Purpose:
Develop creativity, brain-power-boosting brain break, enhancing readiness to focus & learn

Grades:
Preschool through second

Duration:
Two to six minutes – start with two or three minutes and increase duration as ready for it – always keep them wanting more

Equipment Needed:
None

How To:

1. Tell the children that we are going to play a fun game. Say something such as, "I'll ask you: 'Do you see what I see?' You'll reply: 'No, Miss Jones, what do you see'? Then, I'll tell you what I 'see' and then you get to pretend to do what I said I saw."

2. Have students practice the verbal part of this game (i.e., orally replying correctly to your question).

3. Example Teacher: "Do you see what I see?" Students: "No, Miss Jones, what do you see?" Teacher: "I see boys and girls playing basketball – shooting, dribbling, passing the ball..." At this point the students mimic playing basketball while staying right next to their desks.

4. After 10, 15 or 20 seconds, whatever seems appropriate, the teacher says, "Do you see what I see?" After the kids respond verbally, as before, the teacher might say, "I see frogs jumping all over the room." The students then start jumping around the room imitating frogs.

5. Continue in this fashion for an appropriate period of time. Some of the endless possibilities are: playing baseball, moving slowly like turtles, kicking a soccer ball, tightrope walking, clowns in circus, monsters, Superheroes, robots, driving a car, eating popcorn while watching a movie, building something with hammer and nails, dancing...

Tips:

Directions can be to stay next to one's desk or to move around room without touching anyone. This is a great spontaneous activity to use when students need a break from seated activities.

Optional: Play some lively music to energize the class.

Modify to meet your needs or the needs of individual students. For example, a student who has just returned from being sick can stay seated and still pretend to dribble and shoot baskets, or 'bounce' in seat and make frog sounds, etc.

Note: This can be a small group activity, a whole class activity or even a single child's game.

Can You Do This?

Purpose:

Develop spatial-visual skill, ability to follow directions, brain-power-boosting brain break, enhancing readiness to focus & learn

Grades:
Preschool through second

Duration:
Two to six minutes – start with two or three minutes and increase duration as ready for it – always keep them wanting more

Equipment Needed:
None

How To:

1. Tell the children that we are going to play a fun game. Say something such as, "I'll ask you: 'Can you do this?'" Then tell the class that you will then show them a physical action, such as hopping on one foot. Next instruct them that after they've watched your physical action, THEY will reply: 'You mean THIS, Mr. Mayhew?' Then, they get to do their best to imitate the movements you showed them.

2. Have students practice the verbal part of this game (i.e., orally replying in unison to your question).

3. Sample Teacher: "Can you do this?" Teacher does jumping jacks. Students: "You mean THIS, Mr. Mayhew?" As soon as they have finished asking their required question, they start doing jumping jacks to the best of their ability. Do not correct those doing the jumping jacks incorrectly – this is a game, not a lesson.

4. After 10, 15 or 20 seconds, whatever seems appropriate, the teacher says, "Can you do this?" and demonstrates a new movement, such as a kicking the feet while

turning a circle. After the kids respond verbally, "You mean THIS Mr. Mayhew?" -- they attempt to kick while circling.

5. Continue in this fashion for an appropriate period of time. Some of the endless possibilities are: burpees, push-ups, clapping patterns, 180-degree jump turns, jump and click heels in air, jumping side to side, balancing on one foot with eyes open or closed...

Tips:

Directions can be to stay next to one's desk or to move around the room without touching anyone on purpose or by accident (for locomotor challenges). This is a great spontaneous activity to use when students need a break from seated activities.

Optional: Play some lively music to energize the class.

Modify to meet your needs or the needs of individual students. For example, a student who has just returned from being sick can stay seated and still move the arms and/or legs gently in different patterns, etc.

Note: This can be a small group activity, a whole class activity or even a single child's game.

Find Brain Sprints videos at:
YouTube.com, enter "Brain Sprints Math"
or "Ed Mayhew Brain Sprints" or visit
SmarterStrongerChildren.com

CHAPTER SIX

Squat to Learn

Many, if not most, of our children spend hours in front of an electronic screen each and every day. This sedentary lifestyle is interfering with their emotional, social, physical and mental development. By getting them up and moving in the classroom we can give them some of the brain-power-boosting and overall well-being-enhancing physical activity they are missing and maybe instill in them the lifelong habit of taking frequent movement breaks that will help them stay mentally sharp and physically healthy for a lifetime.

Squats are one of the best exercises one can do because they engage some of the largest muscles in one's body for optimal benefits. They are also very easy to implement right in the classroom and the home. Here are five fabulous brain-power-boosting and overall well-being-enhancing Brain Sprints that utilize the awesome power of squats.

The Elevator Game

Purpose:
Counting, alphabet, fractions, brain-power-boosting brain break, enhancing readiness to focus & learn

Grades:
Kindergarten through second

Duration:
One to five minutes – start with a minute or so and increase duration as ready for it – always keep them wanting more

Equipment Needed:
A vertical list of numbers, letters or fractions displayed on a SMART board, dry-erase board, flip chart..., OPTIONAL: music and music player

How To:
1. Display a list of sequential numbers (e.g., 0 to 5) one above the other and draw a tall rectangle around them representing a skyscraper.

2. Show the rectangle and numbers to the kids and tell them this is a tall building and the numbers represent the floors of the building (e.g., 1 is floor 1 or the first floor). Then tell them that they are going to have fun playing the elevator game

3. Have them get into a full squat and pretend there is an elevator in front of them. Have them, while staying in the full squat, pretend to push the button for the elevator doors to open and once in the elevator, make believe they

are pushing the buttons for floors 1, 2, 3, 4 and 5. Make sound effects for each button pushed (e.g., beep, beep...)

4. As you pretend the elevator is rising have them slowly rise, stopping at each floor and saying the number. That is, from the full squat they and you (or a chosen student leader) rise and stop in one-fifth increments for this counting from 1 to 5 example. The students rise from the full squat (the basement) to standing tall and on tip toes on the top floor. Have them look out from the top floor to see the imaginary scenery.

5. Lead them slowly back down as you and they count backwards while stopping at each floor until they arrive back in a full squat as they say "0" or "basement".

6. Repeat this riding of the elevator for two or three more times.

Tips:

Try starting at different floors instead of the basement (e.g., start at floor 6 and go to 10). Use the Elevator Game to practice counting forward and backwards by 2's, 5's and 10's, too. Or the numbers can be replaced by letters as they learn the alphabet. Remember the elevator music.

FRACTIONS: Instead of whole numbers, fractions can be used. Let's use fourths. Have them rise up one fourth of the way, then two fourths, etc. When they get to the top it's four fourths or one whole trip up the elevator. Then reverse and come down to three fourths...At two fourths, you can also say one half way up or down the building. Add eighths and they can start to understand that one fourth equals or is the same distance up the building as two eighths is. Don't try to explain this to prelogical kids; just let those that are ready figure it out for themselves.

If a student can't squat because of an injured leg or whatever, maybe he can participate in his chair by raising and lowering his arms and counting with the rest of the class.

The Blastoff Game

Purpose:
Counting, alphabet, brain-power-boosting brain break, enhancing readiness to focus & learn

Grades:
Kindergarten through second

Duration:
One to three minutes – start with a minute or so and increase duration as ready for it – always keep them wanting more

Equipment Needed:
OPTIONAL – A vertical list of numbers displayed on a SMART board, dry-erase board, flip chart..., OPTIONAL: music and music player

How To:
1. OPTIONAL: Display a list of sequential numbers (e.g., 5, 4 ,3, 2, 1, Blastoff) one above the other with the number "5" at the top and "Blastoff" at the bottom

2. Tell the kids that we are going to play the Blastoff Game and that they are going to pretend to be rockets.

3. Start with each student standing with arms overhead, fingers touching to form the pointed nose of the rocket.

4. Have them slowly lower into a deep squat while counting backwards from five to one.

5. When they get to zero, instead of saying zero they say, "BLASTOFF!" as they leap into the air. Have them continue bouncing up and down a few times while clapping hands overhead to represent the rocket flying through space

Tips:

By counting backwards by different numbers (e.g., by 2's, 5's, 10's starting at 10, 25 and 50 respectively) the sessions can last longer without their losing interest. If you want to include counting forwards, have them start in a squat position, instead of the standing start, and rise up slowly as they count forward (representing the rocket's being put up on the launching pad) and then go lower with the backwards counting part....Remember, playing music can add excitement, too.

If a student can't squat and jump because of an injured leg or whatever, maybe she can participate in her chair by raising and lowering her arms and counting with the rest of the class.

Smart Tiger Squats

Purpose:

Various academics, reading, brain-power-boosting brain break, enhancing readiness to focus & learn

Grades:

Kindergarten through fifth and up depending on the youngster(s) or group

Duration:

One to three minutes – start with a minute or so and increase duration as ready for it – always keep them wanting more

Equipment Needed:

OPTIONAL – A list of words displayed on a SMART board, dry-erase board, flip chart..., OPTIONAL: music and music player

How To:

1. OPTIONAL: Display a list of words /related items to be learned and practiced (e.g., a listing of the 8 planets starting with the one closest to the Sun and working outward)

2. Skip the list if you want them to use and test their memory.

3. LEARNING THE MOVEMENT: Start in a standing position with the arms straight out at shoulder level (like a person sleepwalking typically has his arms) except with palms up and hands making fists. The movement begins with vigorously pulling the arms back towards the body and briefly stopping with the hands close to the ribs on each side. During this pulling in of the arms the student forcefully says, "BOOM!" Then the youngster TAKES ONE BIG BREATH IN while lowering into a deep squat and rising back up to standing position all the while circling the arms back to the starting position. The arm circling is an underhanded large half circle that takes the hands down beside and then well below the knees and continues forward and up to the standing 'sleep-walking' starting position (sort of like the underhand-pitching arm motion of a softball pitcher, but with two arms circling). REPEAT

4. ADDING THE ACADEMICS: Each time the arms are aggressively brought back to the body, the child replaces the word "BOOM" with the next word in the list of words/answers. For learning or practicing the names of the Great Lakes, for instance, it would go like this. Pull arms in and say, "HURON!" After another inhalation, squat and half circle of the arms and while pulling the arms in towards the ribs a second time, say, "ONTARIO!" Next comes "MICHIGAN!" etc. In this fashion, it finishes with 'THESE" "ARE" "THE' 'GREAT" "LAKES" (i.e. one single word stated with each pulling in of the arms).

Tips:
Optional: Playing music can greatly enhance this very powerful brain-power-boosting and overall-well-being-enhancing *Smart Tiger Squat*.

If a student can't squat because of an injured leg or whatever, maybe she can participate in her chair by pulling in and circling her arms and saying the list of words with the rest of the class.

Super-Learning Squats

Purpose:
Various academics, calming effect, brain-power-boosting brain break, enhancing readiness to focus & learn

Grades:
First through fifth and up depending on the youngster(s) or group

Duration:

One to three minutes – start with a minute or so and increase duration as ready for it – always keep them wanting more

Equipment Needed:

OPTIONAL – A list of words, questions, equations...displayed on a SMART board, dry-erase board, flip chart..., OPTIONAL: music and music player

How To:

1. OPTIONAL: Display a list of words, questions, equations...to be learned and practiced

2. Skip the list if you want them to focus mostly on their listening and thinking skills

3. LEARNING THE MOVEMENT: The three parts of this movement (i.e., the breathing, the arm/hand positioning & the squatting) should be practiced separately and then combined. First practice breathing in through the nose and out through the mouth with deep slow breaths. Next practice crossing the arms in front of the chest and holding the ear lobes (i.e., fingers and thumb of left hand holding right ear lobe while the fingers and thumb of the right hand hold the left ear lobe). Finally, with feet shoulder width or wider apart, squat down until the thighs are about horizontal with the floor with upper body leaning forward a little and the back straight, and then rise back up to the standing position. When these three parts have been learned, combine them (i.e., holding the ears throughout, lower into squat position while breathing in through the nose and then breath out through the mouth while rising back to standing position).

4. ADDING THE ACADEMICS: While the students are slowly lowering into their squat position and breathing in through their noses, the teacher states a problem for them to solve which may or may not be visually represented. Then the students vocally give the answer as they rise back up from the squat. The teacher asks, for example, what is the third planet from the Sun and the kids say the answer three times as they rise from squat (i.e., in this example, the students say, "Earth, Earth, Earth!" as they rise up). This works well for math equations, questions about a story just read, definitions for words, science topics...

Tips:

Optional: Playing calming music can greatly enhance this very powerful brain-power-boosting and overall-well-being-enhancing academically-infused *Super Learning Squats*.

Holding the ears has several benefits, but for now let's just tell the kids that holding the ears is a strong reminder to have their ears listen carefully during this "game."

If a student can't squat because of an injured leg or whatever, maybe she can participate in her chair by holding her ears, following the breathing pattern and answering in sync with the rest of the class.

Supercharged Squats

Purpose:

Math equations, counting, spelling, brain-power-boosting brain break, enhancing readiness to focus & learn

Grades:

Second through fifth and up depending on the youngster(s) or group

Duration:

One to three minutes – start with a minute or so and increase duration as ready for it – always keep them wanting more

Equipment Needed:

A list of words, equations...displayed on a SMART board, dry-erase board, flip chart..., OPTIONAL: music and music player

How To:

1. Display a list of words, math equations...to be learned, spelled and practiced

2. LEARNING THE MOVEMENT: This movement can be performed with the assistance of a chair or without one. We'll describe the chair version. Start in a squatting position with one's backside or upper legs lightly touching the front edge of the seat of the chair. The feet are slightly more than shoulder width apart with the upper torso leaning slightly forward, back straight and weight over the feet. Rise up to standing position and touch one elbow to a raised opposite knee. Return to standing on both feet (feet wide apart) and immediately lower till backside or upper back of legs are LIGHTLY touching the chair again. Immediately rise up to standing position and touch the other elbow to its opposite raised knee. Return to starting squat position. REPEAT

3. ADDING THE ACADEMICS: When using the Supercharged Squats to practice basic math facts / equations,

say the numbers while touching elbows to knees and say the words "plus," "minus," "times" or "divided by" and "equals" while touching backside to chair; the exception to this is with the answer (i.e., for single-syllable answers such as 9, 9 is said twice – once with elbow-to-knee touch and again while backside touches chair; for multi-syllable answers, such as twenty-four, the number is divided into two parts, that is, "twenty-" is said while elbow touches knee and then the final syllable "-four" is said while backside is touching chair). With spelling, letters are stated when elbow touch knees and nothing is said when chair is touched. Finish spelling with "spells" as touch one elbow to knee and then naming the word spelled as touch other elbow to knee.

Tips:

Optional: Playing appropriate music can greatly enhance these very powerful brain-power-boosting and over-all-well-being-enhancing *Supercharged Squats*.

Make sure students don't sit on the chair when they squat as the chair can slide out from under them causing a fall. REMIND THEM OFTEN TO TOUCH CHAIR LIGHTLY AT BOTTOM OF EACH SQUAT. If they have trouble just lightly touching their chairs (i.e., not sitting on the chairs), these can be done without chairs. The chairs usually help to make sure that they are squatting deeply enough to get maximum exercise/benefit and without going into a full squat.

If a student can't do these squats because of an injured leg or whatever, maybe she can participate by touching elbows to opposing knees or bending and straightening from the waist while seated in her chair and reciting the answers along with the rest of the class.

**Find Brain Sprints videos at:
YouTube.com, enter "Brain Sprints Math"
or "Ed Mayhew Brain Sprints" or visit
SmarterStrongerChildren.com**

CHAPTER SEVEN

Racing in the Classroom & Home to Learn

When our children exercise, their muscles release a protein, cathepsin b, which travels to the brain where its role is essential for the growth of new brain cells in a major learning and memory part of the brain – the hippocampus. This is just one of dozens of brain-power-boosting, overall well-being-enhancing bio-chemicals that are unleashed in and into their brains when we get them up and moving with Brain Sprints.

Running and racing are not appropriate in the classroom and one's house for obvious reasons. These Brain Sprints, however, make it possible for our youngsters to enjoy races involving high-intensity physical activity safely and advantageously right in the classroom or home. Kids love to run, chase and race. The good feeling emotions of these alternative races helps students learn the attached academics better and to be better, more focused learners in the minutes that follow.

The Great Classroom Race I

Purpose:
Counting, spelling, math equations, brain-power-boosting brain break, enhancing readiness to focus & learn

Grades:
Second through fifth and up depending on the youngster(s) or group

Duration:
One to three minutes – start with a minute or so and increase duration as ready for it – always keep them wanting more

Equipment Needed:
A list of counting-by numbers, words, equations...displayed on a SMART board, dry-erase board, flip chart..., a timer, OPTIONAL: music and music player

How To:

1. Display a list of, words to be spelled or equations to be recited, For counting-by numbers, make three sets of numbers; taking counting by sevens as our example: Set One – 7, 14,...to 84; Set Two – 7, 14...to 84; Set Three 7, 14...to 84

2. LEARNING THE SEATED SUPERCHARGER: While seated reach across the body and touch a bent elbow to the opposite raised bent knee. Return foot to floor and arm to natural side of body while raising the other knee and touching it with its opposing elbow. It's a seated version of the Supercharger with the elbows touching the knees. Practice until this movement is mastered before adding academics.

3. ADDING THE ACADEMICS: Only count on one side and not on the other (e.g., count only when the right elbow touches the left knee). Practice in unison as a class. Don't race until have mastered this at cruising speed.

4. RACING - COUNTING: Give them 20 to 30 seconds to see how far they can count. By having three identical sets of counting by a given number, such as 7s, they can see how far they got in the first set, the second set or the third one in the set number of seconds (e.g., got to 14 in second set might be someone's score during a 20 second time limit). After a rest period (e.g., maybe doing a written assignment for 10 or 15 minutes) have them race again to see if they can beat their score. Later, repeat with a third race (a second chance to set a new personal best). The reward is the good feeling of setting a new record and can be enhanced with a brief silent celebration and perhaps by keeping a written record of their achievements.

5. RACING – SPELLING: Give them one minute to see how many words from a numbered list of words they can spell. Their score is the number of the last word they spelled. Like the counting, only say letters with the elbow-to-knee touches on one side. Include parts of

words for improvement / setting new records (e.g., race #1 – reached 3rd letter in 5th word; race #2 reached 6th letter of 5th word)

6. RACING – EQUATIONS: Give them one minute to see how many equations they can complete. Again, one side only (e.g. each time touch left knee say next number or word in the equation: seven; times; four; equals; twenty-; -eight). Include parts of equations for improvement / setting new records (e.g., race #1 – reached 1st number in 4th equation; race #2 reached equals sign in 4th equation)

IMPORTANT: Practice in unison, as a group, until seated-supercharger pattern combined with academic component is mastered before racing! Make sure students are touching elbows to knees and not wrists or forearms to thighs or knees.

Tips:

Optional: Play upbeat music to energize the class for this very powerful brain-power-boosting and overall-well-being-enhancing seated Supercharger and its races.

Emphasize that this is a race to see if one can improve on his/her own previous score and deemphasize competing against classmates.

If a student can't do the elbow-to-knee movement because of an injured leg, clothing issue or whatever, modify the movement for her.

The Great Classroom Race II

Purpose:
Counting, spelling, math equations, brain-power-boosting brain break, enhancing readiness to focus & learn

Grades:
Second through fifth and up depending on the youngster(s) or group

Duration:
One to three minutes – start with a minute or so and increase duration as ready for it – always keep them wanting more

Equipment Needed:
A list of counting-by numbers, words, equations...displayed on a SMART board, dry-erase board, flip chart..., a timer, OPTIONAL: music and music player

How To:

1. Display a list of, words to be spelled or equations to be recited, For counting-by numbers, make three sets of numbers; taking counting by nines as an example: Set One – 9, 18,...to 108; Set Two – 9, 18...to 108; Set Three – 9, 18...to 108

2. LEARNING THIS MORE CHALLENGING SUPER-CHARGER: Have skip in place beside desks with knees lifted high so that the top of the thighs alternately reach about waist high and parallel with the floor. When the left leg is raised, reach across the body and touch the

elbow of the right arm to the knee of the raised leg. Then as the right leg raises reach across the body similarly and touch its knee with the left elbow. REPEAT this pattern. Make sure that the arm not engaged (i.e., the one not reaching across body) is returned to its natural side of the body after each touch. It's another version of the Supercharger (Visit SmarterStronger-Children.com for VIDEO of regular Supercharger). Practice until this movement is mastered before adding academics.

3. ADDING THE ACADEMICS: Only count on one side and not on the other (e.g., count only when the right elbow touches the left knee). Practice in unison as a class first. Don't race until have mastered this at cruising speed.

4. RACING - COUNTING: Give them 20 to 30 seconds to see how far they can count. By having three identical sets of counting by a given number, such as counting by 9s, they can see how far they got in the first set, the second set or the third (e.g., got to 18 in second set might be someone's score). After a rest period (e.g., doing a written assignment for 10 or 15 minutes) have them race again to see if they can beat their score. For each race they start at the beginning of the first set. The reward is the good feeling of setting a new record and can be enhanced with a silent celebration. How about a third race to set a new personal best?

5. RACING – SPELLING: Give them one minute to see how many words from a numbered list of words they can spell. Their score is the number of the last word they spelled. Like the counting, only say letters with the elbow-to-knee touches on one side. Longer words

may require a greater time limit (e.g., 90 seconds, two minutes ...). Include parts of words for improvement / setting new records (e.g., race #1 – reached 3rd letter in 5th word; race #2 reached 6th letter of 5th word)

6. RACING – EQUATIONS: Give them one minute to see how many equations they can complete. Again, one side only (e.g., each time touch left knee, they say next number or word in the equation: nine; times; six; equals; fifty-; -four). Important to practice in unison as a group until pattern is mastered before racing. Include parts of equations for improvement / setting new records (e.g., race #1 – reached 1st number in 4th equation; race #2 reached equals sign in 4th equation)

Tips:

Optional: Play upbeat music to energize the class and supercharge this very powerful brain-power-boosting and over-all-well-being-enhancing version of the *Supercharger* and its races.

Make sure students are touching elbow bone to the knee bone and not forearms or wrists to thighs, for example. Always practice this more advanced *Supercharger* without the academics first and then combined with the academics, as a whole class and in unison, before doing any racing.

Emphasize that this is a race to see if one can improve on his/her own previous score and deemphasize competing against classmates.

If a student can't do this Supercharger because of an injured leg, clothing issue or whatever, he may be able to do a seated version and vocally follow along with the counting, spelling or equations.

Jog, Jump 'n Brainstorm

Purpose:
To practice & improve divergent thinking / brainstorming, brain-power-boosting brain break, enhance readiness to focus & learn

Grades:
Kindergarten to sixth grade and up depending on the youngster(s) or group (e.g., groups of adults greatly enjoy this, too)

Duration:
30 seconds to one minute of brainstorming Brain Sprints' style, then rest, discuss and repeat – Total time with discussion phase, 3 to 10 minutes– always keep them wanting more

Equipment Needed:
A timer; OPTIONAL: upbeat music and player

How To:
Give the students a brainstorming task (e.g., think of ways to get from point A to point B; the two points can be close together, as in the distance across the room, or very far apart, for example, hundreds of miles apart). Challenge them to see how many different answers they can name within a given time limit, such as 30 seconds. Have students continuously jog in place beside their desks (interrupted only by the jumps) throughout the 30-second *Jog, Jump 'n Brainstorm* session. For an example, one of the students might start by saying, "one – car!" More precisely, this child says, "one" while jogging and jumps up and claps his hands a single time over

head, while saying "car" at the top of the jump. He/she then continues jogging and while saying, "two" (and thinking of another answer) and then jumps up again and says, "train," for example. Each child continues in this fashion, jogging while numbering and thinking and then jumping up and giving his/her own unique answer. When you say stop, each youngster will have a certain number of answers – a score. Conduct a brief discussion of answers and then challenge the students to see if each can improve his/her score. Maybe, as their reward, direct them to do a silent cheer if they beat their previous record.

Tips:

Note: Unlike the *Jog, Jump 'n Learn* activities in chapter one which use triple jumps, in the *Jog, Jump 'n Brainstorm* the participants only JUMP UP A SINGLE TIME WITH EACH ANSWER. However, if they've gotten used to three jumps from previously performing the *Jog, Jump 'n Learn* activities, then sticking with the three-jump protocol may be easier than trying to unlearn the 3-jump *habit*.

Remind students to mentally record and REMEMBER their scores. Emphasize the fun and challenge of trying to beat one's own personal best, as opposed to attempting to compete with peers. That way everyone has a good chance to win and the possibility of arguments is greatly lessened.

Optional: Put on some upbeat music to energize the class.

Modify to meet your needs or the needs of individual students. For example, a student who has just returned from being sick, can stay seated and pump his arms like he's running and clap his hands overhead during the jumping action.

Have a time for discussion after each timed challenge. Congratulate students for giving unique answers and encourage others to do the same. Give them some examples of more original ideas (e.g., for the above challenge you might say, did anyone think of stilt walking, wind surfing, rocket...?) How about a writing and/or drawing assignment describing their favorite answer(s) and why?

A *Jog, Jump 'n Brainstorm* session *is* a great way to start a creative writing class, to come up with alternative endings to a story that was just read, or to use whenever your youngsters need a break from seated activities. It really is as simple as finding a challenge (e.g., explore uses for a piece of rope; name as many foods as you can that would make/keep you healthy and strong; what could you do with a sock besides wear it on your foot?...), having the kids stand up beside their desks and start jogging, numbering and jumping up to joyfully exclaim their ideas. And then there's the fun and exercise of seeing if they can beat their record. The kids are sure to love it and you for having them do it!

Fast Feet

Purpose:
Basic math facts/equations, brain-power-boosting brain break, readiness to focus & learn enhancing

Grades:
Third through sixth and up depending on the youngster(s) or group

Duration:
One to three minutes – start with a minute or so and increase duration as ready for it – always keep them wanting more

Equipment Needed:

A lettered list of math equations...displayed on a SMART board, dry-erase board, flip chart..., OPTIONAL: music and music player

How To:

1. Display a list of sequential math equations, such as the times table for threes (e.g., 0 x 3 = 0...to 12 x 3 = 36)

2. LEARNING FAST FEET: Fast Feet is merely hop-scotching in place. First, practice straddle jumping (i.e., the jumping jacks' leg movements without the arm action—legs jumping apart and then together). After they show good mastery of the straddle jumps, modify to landing on one foot and then the other WHEN THE FEET COME TOGETHER. Starting position is standing with feet a little more than shoulder width apart; jump feet together landing on right foot; jump feet apart and land on both feet (i.e., starting position); jump feet together landing on left foot; jump feet apart and land on both feet (i.e., starting position). It doesn't matter whether they use the right or left foot first. The reason this four-jump pattern is so difficult for some students to learn is because it requires the two brain hemispheres to give two different directives SIMULTANEOUSLY. Because the left hemisphere controls the right leg and the right hemisphere controls the left leg, Fast Feet will improve coordination/communication between the hemispheres for better whole brain learning.

3. ADDING THE ACADEMICS: Let's use three's times table, for an example, starting with 3 x 0 = 0. Start with feet wide apart in straddle position. Jump, bringing feet in and landing on one foot while saying, "3"; jump

the feet apart and land on both feet as say, "times"; jump, bringing feet together and landing on the other foot while saying, "o"; jump feet apart and say, "equals"; jump on first foot while saying, "ze-"; jump on both feet while saying, "-ro" Note: When the ANSWER is multi-syllable we break it into two parts, as above; when the ANSWER is a single syllable word, we say the answer twice. Printed in shorthand, 3 x 0 = 0 and 3 x 1 = 3 look like this (B = Both Feet / straddle; R = Right Foot; L = Left Foot): Starting with standing on B – R "3" – B "times" – L "0" – B "equals" – R "ze-" – B "-ro" - R "3"-- B "times" – L "1" – B "equals" – R "3" – B "3"

4. Before racing, have practice together (as a whole class) taking them slowly through the movement sans equations and then performing Fast Feet with the equations. Finally, have them practice independently without and then with the equations as you help those needing assistance, and encourage them to practice at home.

5. RACING - EQUATIONS: Once they've mastered the Fast Feet with the equations, give them 20 seconds to a minute to see how many equations they can complete. Their score is how many equations (and parts of equations) they complete in the given time limit. If students get to the end of the list of equations before time is up, have them start over from the beginning (in this case their score might be 3 x 5 = 15 the second time through). After a rest period (e.g. doing a written assignment for 10 or 15 minutes) have them race again to see if they can beat their score. The reward is the good feeling of setting a new record and can be enhanced with a silent celebration. How about a third race to set a new personal best?

Tips:

Optional: Play lively music to energize the class.

Make sure students have mastered the *Fast Feet* pattern with and without the equations before any racing. Emphasize that this is a race to see if one can improve on his/her own previous score and deemphasize competing against classmates.

If a student can't do the *Fast Feet* because of an injured leg or whatever, he may be able to do a seated version, maybe touching the floor lightly with his feet, while following along with reciting the equations.

**Find Brain Sprints videos at:
YouTube.com, enter "Brain Sprints Math"
or "Ed Mayhew Brain Sprints" or visit
SmarterStrongerChildren.com**

CHAPTER EIGHT

And There's More

Scientists at the University of Loughborough, in England, put subjects on stationary bikes and had them sprint as fast as they could for 30 seconds. This SINGLE short session of exercise caused their human growth hormone (Hgh) levels to rise 530% above baseline and stay up for a couple of hours. Hgh signals the release of bio-chemicals known as growth factors which grow the body bigger and stronger (e.g. heart, lungs, bones...) and are responsible for growing new brain cells and their supporting new blood vessels in the learning and memory part of the brain. Many of the Brain Sprints in this book can supply this brain-power-boosting high-intensity exercise that too many of our children are missing.

We have emphasized the fact that most of these **Brain Sprints** learning activities give youngsters some of the missing Moderate-to-Vigorous Physical Activity that they need. This is of utmost importance because this is the first generation of children where a significant number of them are living a sedentary lifestyle due to advances in technology. Concerning this, a 2018 NPAP report determined that less than half, just 46.5%, of American children, ages 6 to 17, get the daily 60 minutes of MVPA needed to be their best.

As we can see from this chapter's lead-in, it doesn't take much high-intensity exercise to make a big difference. The key is to get the youngsters to perform the sprinting-in-place and jumping activities with high energy and as much effort as possible. In this regard, getting the knees up about waist high, as well as going as fast as they can during the sprints, is most beneficial.

Brain Sprints – Much More than Mere Exercise

There are several factors that make Brain Sprints the best brain breaks for the classroom and home besides the obvious brain-power-boosting and overall well-being-enhancing exercise component:

- Most engage visual, auditory, tactile/kinesthetic and vocalization modes of learning SIMULTANEOUSLY

- The NOVELTY of combining academic material with unique movement activities and combinations of physical activities wakes up the brain for learning

- Include the REPETITION that we and our children need for enhanced recall

- Engage the EMOTIONS which improves the retention of the academics

- Teacher/parent have freedom to CHOOSE which academic material to combine with most of the Brain Sprints

- EASY TO IMPLEMENT right in the classroom and home, right next to their desks
- Some include unique physical activities (think, SUPER-CHARGER) that improve the coordination and communication between the brain hemispheres for improved whole brain learning
- NO LOSS OF ACADEMIC TIME as curriculum items are part of these "brain breaks"
- NO COST – no giant balls to sit on, no new PE equipment to buy, no scheduling headaches trying to fit in more gym and recess time

AND, of course, there is the flood of brain-power-boosting, body-building bio-chemicals unleashed *in* the brain and *into* the brain by the EXERCISE component.

Brain Sprints Evolve

Yours truly was experimenting with early versions of the Brain Sprints, called Mathletics at the time, in and around 1990. Many new brain-power boosters have evolved since then and others have faded away as we've been working with them in classes ever since. New additions and modifications will continue to come forth (as I'm still in the classrooms regularly after 52 years of teaching) to help children to be their best in the classroom and at home. Some of these improvements may be your ideas.

The Brain Sprints
Card Game

Here's a simple but powerful Brain Sprints learning activity that I almost forgot to include. Make a series of large cards (maybe 4" x 10") out of poster board or foamboard. Print a word or two on each card. Put on some lively music and instruct the youngsters to move according to what the card says, while staying next to their desks or in one spot.

For example, if the word on the card is "jump," they jump up and down all the while saying, "jump, jump, jump..." until you show them another word/card. Here are a few word/activity choices:

Run / run in place

Popcorn / bounce like popcorn being popped

Kick / pretend to kick a soccer ball

Elevator / slowly lower into a squat and back up

Balance / balance on one foot

Stop / stop

Others: Stand up – Sit down – Go faster – Slower – Frogs – Baseball – the possibilities are endless

For best results, remind the students to say the word AND look at the word while doing the associated movement activity. Start with just three cards and gradually add words/cards as ready. Have fun with this. It's a great activity for those young readers and those learning a second language.

Backwards Jeopardy
Latest Addition to Brain Sprints

The newest member of the Brain Sprints family is *Backwards Jeopardy*. The great thing about this brain-power booster is it is so easy for teachers and parents to implement and yet so profoundly powerful for children's learning. To benefit from this activity, one simply makes a list of two to five categories / words displayed on a dry-erase board, flip chart...and mentally comes up with or puts down in writing some items that fit into each category. Let's look at some examples of how *Backwards Jeopardy* can be used.

Backwards Jeopardy
for Reading Comprehension

Reading Comprehension Example:
The children are finishing up an assignment at their desks and need a break from the seated work. Since the teacher has recently read *Jack and the Beanstalk* to the kids, she decides to use it as the subject of a *Backwards Jeopardy* brain break. The teacher puts the following list of categories on the board: Jack – Beanstalk – Giant – None of the Above.

She challenges the students to match the information from Jack and the Beanstalk that she is about to name with one of the categories/words listed on the board. Then she asks them to stand, puts on some spirited music and asks them to jog in place during the entire activity except for when they jump up three times, saying the answer with each jump

(See Chapter 1's *Jog, Jump 'n Learn* for detailed instructions for the jogging and jumping).

Teacher says: Grew tall overnight

Students jump and say: Beanstalk, beanstalk, beanstalk

Teacher says: Owned a goose

Students jump and say: Giant, giant, giant

Teacher says: traded magic beans for a cow

Students jump up and say: Jack, Jack, Jack

Teacher says: Wrong. Jack traded the cow for the beans, not the beans for a cow. The answer should have been None of the Above

Teacher says: Chopped down the beanstalk

Students jump up and say: Jack, Jack, Jack

And so forth...

Backwards Jeopardy

for History

History Example:

While students are finishing up an assignment, teacher puts the following war categories on the board:

WWI – Revolutionary War – WWII – Civil War.

Here is a sampling of some of the information about these wars that the students could try to match with the four war categories:

1914 – 1918; General Eisenhower; President Abraham Lincoln; General George Washington; colonies vs. Britain; North vs. South; Pearl Harbor...

Backwards Jeopardy
for Science

Science Example:
While students are finishing up an assignment, teacher puts the following biology categories on the board:

Mammals – Marsupials – Amphibians – Reptiles

Here is a sampling of some of the animals that the students could try to match with the four categories of animals:

Cows; Snakes; Kangaroos; Frogs; Whales; Lizards; Man...

Backwards Jeopardy
for Math

Math Example:
While students are finishing up an assignment, teacher puts the following numbers/categories on the board:

4 – 8 – 12 – None of the Above

Here is a sampling of some of the math the youngsters could do to see if the answers to their math computations match one or none of the three numbers/categories:

$3 + 1 = $ ___; $9 - 1 = $ ___; $4 + 8 = $ ___; $3 \times 4 = $ ___; $(8 \times 2) - 12 = $ ___; $1 + 2 + 4 + 1 = $ ___; $20 + 13 = $ ___...

Tips:
Optional: Play lively music to energize the class and enhance interest.

There is no limit to the curriculum categories that can be used to enhance learning through frequent use of *Backwards Jeopardy*. From reading comprehension to health to science to social studies, just put up two to five categories on the board and you are ready for a powerful brain-power-boosting brain break any time you and your students need one.

The *information* to be matched with the two to five categories can be just named by the teacher/parent (highly recommended to improve listening skills) or it can be displayed in written and/or picture form for the students to see. It makes more work for the adult to present this *information* in written form and makes it harder for these sessions to be spontaneous decisions to get the kids up and moving when they need a break from seated activities. The other side of this choice is that additional visual information definitely helps children learn.

If a student can't do the jogging and jumping because of an injured leg or whatever, he can do a seated version, moving the arms as if jogging and raising the arms and clapping hands overhead while vocally making the matches with the rest of the class.

There's More at SmarterStrongerChildren.com...

For videos and more information on the Brain Sprints program for academic excellence, visit SmarterStrongerChildren. com. Or go to YouTube.com or TeacherTube.com and type in "Brain Sprints Math" or "Ed Mayhew Brain Sprints" for some videos featuring our animated cartoon character – *BrainMan*.

Or visit Amazon.com and other booksellers to check out our companion book:

Smarter Stronger Children: The Mega Brain-Power Booster / Muscle Makers Program for Excellence Teacher & Parent Guide

**Find Brain Sprints videos at:
YouTube.com and TeacherTube.
com, enter "Brain Sprints Math" or
"Ed Mayhew Brain Sprints" or visit
SmarterStrongerChildren.com**

**Ed is available for workshops, in-services,
presentations and consultation
Contact through
SmarterStrongerChildren.com**

About the Author

Ed Mayhew created his very successful *Brain Sprints* program based on his 52 years as an educator, during which he worked with school children, teachers and parents to help students achieve excellence. Ed is the author of several books promoting the benefits of physical activity for overall well-being and improved brain power, and has produced videos and audio materials on these subjects. A dynamic presenter, he enjoys sharing his expertise and *Brain Sprints* learning activities with adults and children. He lives in the Shenandoah Valley of Virginia with his wife, Mary.

As a long-time elementary school principal, I've seen firsthand what Ed Mayhew's Mega Brain Power Boosters can do. They flat-out work!

— J. Vernon Laney,
Curriculum Coordinator

I highly recommend Ed Mayhew's Mega Brain Power Boosters/Brain Sprints program. It was well received by the students, teachers, and parents alike...It is an easy and fun way to accelerate academic learning.

— Anita Jenkins,
Elementary School Principal

Ed shared his passion for physical activity and Brain Sprints at our VAESP [Virginia Association of Elementary School Principals] Northern Zone meeting. He had some of the best and brightest principals in the area jogging, jumping, and actively engaged in learning. His data on the correlation between brain activity and physical activity reinforced what we have observed as educators—kids need stimulation to motivate and connect learning. We had a blast! Thanks for sharing how Mega Brain-Power Boosters lead to smarter, stronger children.

— Clark Bowers, Ed.D.,
Northern Zone Director for VAESP

Made in United States
North Haven, CT
01 March 2025

66387524R00114